MW00426913

My Best Friends

Call Me Susan

By Dr. Loretta Long

With Scott Alboum

Edited by Janet Dengel

Copyright © Up Front Productions 2016

Photos used with permission from

Sesame Workshop and The Loretta Long Collection

All rights reserved.

ISBN:1502776324

ISBN-13: 978-1502776327

INTRODUCTION

Like most children growing up in America, I loved watching *Sesame Street*. I can remember growing up in the 1980s without cable and watching it on WNET Channel 13 from New York City. I loved the characters on the show and I connected with them. I learned so much from watching *Sesame Street* and when I look back at old episodes or hear a familiar song it's like traveling through time back to my childhood. Now that I'm a father, I have rediscovered *Sesame Street* and have introduced it to my children. As I started to rediscover the show, I began to pick up some old *Sesame Street* record albums I had owned as a kid at a friend's record shop in Long Island, New York. I hung a few of them up on the wall in my children's playroom that is in the basement of my house in Hamilton, New Jersey. Over time my friend Mark, who owns the record store in Long Island, started to save any *Sesame Street* records he would get for me. One day back in early 2012 he gave me an album called "Susan Sings Songs from *Sesame Street*." It was from 1970 and contained songs sung by Loretta Long who plays Susan on the show. The Children's Chorus of New York accompanied her on the album. I knew I never had this album as a kid mainly because it was from about seven years before I was born. Something about this album intrigued me. Maybe it was the photos on the album cover or the short bio of Loretta Long from the inside of the album jacket. I'm not really sure what it was and, eventually, I just put the record onto my shelf with all of the others in my collection. This one never made it on the wall of the playroom, but I never forgot about it.

When I am not with my family or buying up old *Sesame Street* record albums I am usually working in the television studio at Rider University in Lawrenceville, New Jersey. I run the television studio and teach video production classes in Rider's Department of Communication and Journalism. I am also the advisor to the Rider University Network, a club for students on campus who are interested in producing television shows for our on-campus television station. One day, late in the fall semester of 2012, one of my students stopped by my office with a handwritten letter on *Sesame Street* stationery. It wasn't the kind of thing that happens everyday. The stationery had a caricature of Susan from the show on it and it quickly became clear that it was a note from Loretta Long. It said "Dear Professor, please call me." It listed a bunch of phone numbers and some email addresses to reach her. The moment I saw the caricature of Susan, I instantly remembered the record album I had gotten earlier in the year. Most of the time people seek guys like me out because they are looking for someone to make a video for them for free or something like that. At first I was confused and couldn't understand why someone who has been on television for over forty years would need my help with anything. Then, my student explained to me that Loretta was a woman who frequented a restaurant she worked at and that, over time, they became friends. She told me that I should call Loretta because she wanted someone to help her with a project she was having trouble getting started. My student thought that I was the right kind of person to help her. I nervously picked up the phone on my desk. Since I work at a television station that reaches less then 4,000 people, I usually don't get to talk to television stars on the phone. I dialed one of the numbers that she had written on the stationery. The phone began to ring and, after what seemed to be forever, she answered the phone. Since that day, Loretta Long has been my friend. What you are reading is the project that Loretta wanted me to help her with. She needed someone to help her tell her story and to collect stories from her fellow cast mates and friends about what it was like to work with her over the years on *Sesame Street*. She also wanted to collect stories from viewers of the show and she wanted to document how the show affected their lives. This book tells the story of Loretta Long's life growing up on a farm in Paw

Paw, Michigan, and how she dreamed of a career in show business. It will take you on a journey through her career and how she is still living her dream. I've enjoyed helping her tell her story and I am so happy that I luckily became a part of it.

In this book you are often going to read the words, **It's Time To Occupy Your Dream.** That means you should identify, occupy and live your dream. Those words mean a lot to Loretta and this book is an example of **Occupying Your Dream**. I hope you will enjoy reading Loretta's story as much as I have enjoyed getting to know her over the past few years.

Scott Alboum, Rider University, NJ

Scott and Stacey Alboum with their children: Zoey age 5, and twins Samuel and Alexa age 2 at Sesame Place, June 2015.

This book is dedicated to my parents
Verle and Marjorie Moore.

I'm Loretta Long but my best friends call me Susan…

Sesame Street, Susan "S" and logo are trademarks of Sesame Workshop. All rights reserved.

Most people don't know that I grew up on a farm in Michigan, once auditioned for Berry Gordy at Motown, and that I earned a Doctorate of Education at the University of Massachusetts. They only seem to know one thing about me. I play Susan on the hit children's television show *Sesame Street*. People always recognize me from the show and they think that my name really is Susan, and some people even think that Sesame Street is a real place. Well, my name is really Dr. Loretta Long and I have decided to write this book to tell my story and to let fans of *Sesame Street* also tell their stories at the same time.

Over time, people started telling me their stories. I didn't even catch on to it for a while. People would just stop me and start saying things like, "Susan, you know, when I was little…" and very rarely could I get them to call me Loretta. Even when I was on a college campus and they had signed up for my course, Diversity: The *Sesame Street* Way, they still would walk in the door and say, "Hi, Susan." I would say, "Can you at least call me Dr. Susan so I can get paid?" That became a recurring joke in that course.

Then I began to think about how many times in my life are people going to experience a show as a child and then have a chance to experience it again as an adult maybe through the eyes of their own child? That's an interesting time and space continuum that's just not going to happen again. As an educator, I feel that this special time and space needs to be documented. This book, I think, is a funny, happy way to do that. Even though I wish people would just call me Loretta, I do like hearing the stories from the parents who are now grandparents. I also like the stories from the children who are now all grown up. They are amazing to listen to and in this book I will be sharing some of my favorite stories with you.

I met a young lady, a pretty young woman. She is an actress and she said something very funny to me. She said,

"Go look at Season 25 of *Sesame Street*. I'm the little kid in the red sneakers."

She was on the show. Then she said,

"And I have the poster at home framed."

I said, "Oh, okay. You cleaned up real nice, girl!"

She laughed. To me there's just something so interesting about how people connect to the show in their own way.

A lot of teachers tell me that they are teaching because they fell in love with education on the show. It's overwhelming because, as an actor, you just get up everyday and you go do your job. When you hear these good stories, you realize that you must have done your job well. To me, that means so much and I cherish all of the times that I have met a teacher who has told me that.

One of the most important things to me is my faith. It is the basis of who I am. I come from a family of faith. My great-grandparents were emancipated slaves who had the courage to leave Kentucky and go to Kansas to homestead. It seems that two ministers, one black and one white, spoke in my Great-Granddaddy's church. They read the Homestead Act to the congregation. Great-Grandpa George Moore, Sr. stood up and said,

"This sharecropping sounds like new slavery to me, and the people are meaner than they ever were. I'm going to Kansas where I can own my own field."

You would expect the congregation to cheer. You know what they said?

"What's a Kansas?"

You have to understand that people might have only been down the road to somebody else's plantation and that's it. They all said,

"Kansas? What's a Kansas?"

They didn't even know it was a completely different place.

I took my father on his 97th birthday back to that town, Nicodemus, Kansas. As we were going over the Mississippi River at six in the morning on the train bridge, I looked out and I saw this great big river. I thought of the courage and the faith that my great-grandparents had to have to journey from Kentucky to Kansas. That would be like saying,

"Okay, meet me at Cape Canaveral. We're going off on the Space Shuttle."

That kind of faith is the bedrock of my family, so I was raised with that kind of faith. I know it works because I've seen it work.

If we had a family logo, ours would say, "No whining."

We're homesteaders. We're pioneers. We're people of faith. That gives us the spirit of not quitting.

Everything has to come from a place of love. The stuff that comes from a wounded place is always polluted. I'm always working on coming from a place of love instead of a wounded place. That's the foundation of who I am and led me to who I became.

Part 1: I'm from a place called Paw Paw...

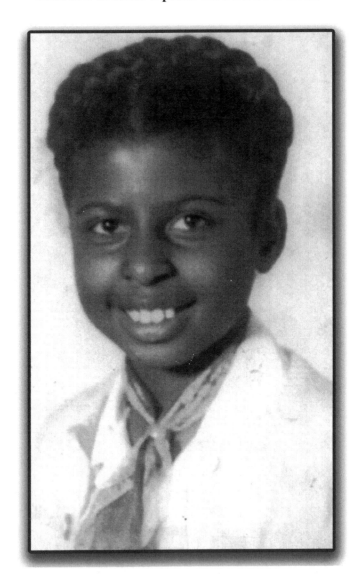

I was seven years old when we moved to a farm in Paw Paw, Michigan from Chicago. My little brother Charles was only five. After World War II, my mother and father saved their money in hopes to have a better life. Back then, Daddy was an aircraft welder. We lived on what is now an Air Force base called Hill Air Force Base, but it was called Hill Field because there wasn't even an Air Force back then. It was the Army Air Corp.

Daddy came from an agrarian background. He was born on a homestead in Kansas. His grandparents were emancipated slaves who helped to found their own town in Kansas. They came from Kentucky and Daddy was born on his father's homestead in Logan County, Kansas. He didn't even have a birth certificate. Actually, no one in his family had a birth certificate. He didn't get one until he was a grown man so that he could pay into the Social Security system and receive Social Security.

He loved life on a farm so much that his dream was to put his kids on a farm to raise them in the country. He didn't like the city, so we eventually moved from Chicago to Michigan. My parents bought a forty-acre farm and we lived and worked there. The joke was always that the slaves were supposed to get forty acres and a mule. Daddy said that he got tired of waiting for his forty acres and a mule, so he bought forty acres and a tractor and kept going. Growing up as kids, we mostly worked that farm. Day in and day out we were working. We raised anything that would grow on a vine and could be put it in a bushel basket. Then we would try to sell it to anyone who would stop by. We lived and worked on a roadside farm and many people would just stop by. They would buy things like tomatoes, cucumbers, strawberries and cantaloupes from us. We really grew anything you could raise on a truck farm. That's what they called it back then. Most of my life in the summer was spent raising crops to sell. It was a lot of work, but that work became the foundation of a very strong work ethic that I have carried with me my entire life.

Along with growing crops, we also had chickens, hogs and cows. We had to get up and do the chores before we took on the rest of our lives. My parents both worked day jobs and my brother and I went to school. We had to do all the chores before the school bus came or else we had the privilege of trying to walk three miles from our house to the school if we missed the bus. We learned to stay focused and work hard and fast.

Back then we didn't watch television like people do today. Entertainment for us was whatever we did for ourselves. My mother and father had this fantastic record collection of old vinyl discs. They had many albums from artists like Nat King Cole. My mother and father were good dancers and they won prizes in dance marathons. So we listened to lots of music, danced and made up routines for fun.

In 2012, my Daddy graduated to heaven at age 98. In his last years he loved to watch the television show *Dancing with the Stars*. When I watched the show with him, he would always say,

"Your mother and I danced for groceries, not some mirror ball."

My parents danced so well. They were jitterbugs, so when my father saw them do the jive on *Dancing with the Stars*, he would laugh and laugh. We all could sing. My father had been a tap dancer, so we all could dance. Singing was my gift and my mother would always say I could sing when I was a baby.

A collection of early photographs of my brother Charlie and I. Daddy carried some of these around in his wallet until the day he graduated to heaven in 2012.

My brother Charlie, my little sister, my mother and me on our family farm in Paw Paw, MI. I am about 12 years old and it's around 1950.

On our new tractor with my mother and my brother on the farm back in Paw Paw, Michigan in the late 1940s.

My little brother Charlie and me all dressed up on Easter Sunday in the late 1940s.

There really wasn't that much of an outlet for a black family in the small white middle America community of Paw Paw, Michigan. There was a small black community in Kalamazoo, Michigan— that's New York Yankee shortstop Derek Jeter's hometown. My parents had some friends who lived there, so they had a little social life outside of Paw Paw. Because we were black that made us outsiders in Paw Paw. We were the city slickers from Chicago. Our family had to be our own unit because we really just didn't socialize in Paw Paw. That strong unit still exists today and I'm so thankful for it.

Back then we watched the radio. I think I was getting ready for television. We would all pull up our chairs and sit and watch the radio. I don't know why, but we'd sit right in front of the radio. That's what everyone did in those days. I drew a lot of inspiration from listening to radio. One program that really inspired me was *Major Bowes' The Original Amateur Hour*. It was like an *American Idol* but for radio. They would bring on all types of unknown singers trying to catch a break and get noticed. I would listen to all the talent contests and dream of being on the show. I'd listen to the singers and say,

"Oh, I could sing better than that one."

I was nine years old out in the field picking cucumbers and knew I didn't want to do that forever. So I would fantasize. I tell kids all the time that they shouldn't be discouraged when their reality doesn't match their dream. I always say, just dream your dream fully. I would be out in the field. My reality would be a bucket, galoshes, Tom Sawyer straw hat, bib overalls and a shirt from Goodwill. But in my mind, I had on a taffeta dress and patent leather Mary Janes. Instead of having my hair in braids, I had Shirley Temple curls and I would hold a microphone instead of a cucumber. I always saw myself performing.

As I grew up and advanced in school, some real singing and performing opportunities came my way. Honestly, the actress part of it really was not happening for me in the beginning. That's because I refused to be a maid or Harriet Tubman. Those were the stereotypical roles that black girls were expected to play in those days. I just wouldn't do it. It was wrong and I knew I could do more than that. So the actress part of it didn't happen then, but I could sing.

There was this lid that people attempted to put on me because I was black and a female; so it wasn't just the racial thing, it was gender too. It was a two-gun salute in that respect. When I think back about racial discrimination and how it affected me, the first thing I really remember was that after sixth grade I no longer had a social life in school. Up to sixth grade, I didn't realize I was different. I was part of the gang. I came from a very, very small school, so we just all did everything together. But by seventh grade, where socialization happened, things started to change for me.

I made a mistake of being on the decorating committee for the seventh grade party, so I had to attend it. I'll never forget sitting and looking at my little ballerina slippers all night long. I wouldn't even look up because no one asked me to dance because I was black and they were all white. The part that really broke my heart was that I had to sit there all night because the decorating committee was also the cleanup committee, so I couldn't even leave. To have to sit there all night and to have no one ask me to dance was heartbreaking.

There was one brave young boy who was my friend. I'll never

forget the knot of seventh grade boys by the boys' gym that was across the dance floor. I was still sitting there looking at my feet. All of a sudden, I heard these squeaky shoes. I started to see these high water pants coming my way; he had outgrown his suit. I looked up and it was John Coleman. He had felt so bad for me sitting there all night long by myself. He built up the courage and he braved that long walk, which was like walking the plank from where the boys were, to ask me to dance. We ended up being the only ones on the dance floor because it was a black girl and a white boy dancing. He was sweating, so his little hands were all sweaty, and he was literally shaking. But how brave of him. I'll never forget that. Honestly, I experienced so many situations where no one stepped forward in the past, so this one just still sticks out in my mind today.

As I moved on to high school, anytime I had a chance to sing, I took it. I sang in the chorus and always competed to sing solos in the high school choir. During that time, I had a music teacher named Will Hahnenburg. He was our choir director but he was really an instrumental teacher. One day, he took me aside and said,

"I really believe that you have enough talent that you could work in this business."

He said, "But I don't want to give you voice lessons because I'm an instrumentalist, and I don't want to mess anything up. But what I can do is offer you a singing job."

This was one of the defining moments in my high school career and the beginning of my career as an entertainer. What confirmation. I went from fifty cents an hour babysitting to fifty dollars a night singing songs like "Moonlight in Vermont."

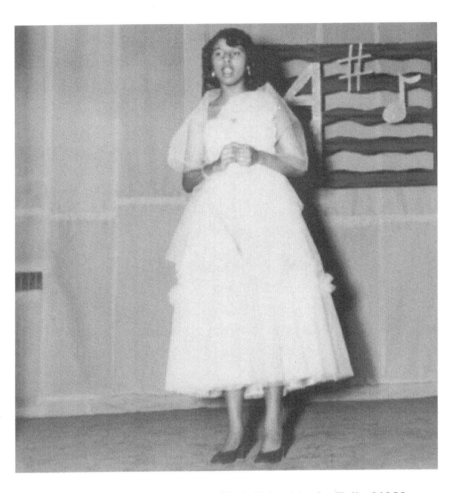

Singing on stage at Paw Paw High School in the Fall of 1955.

This photo was taken on the day I was offered a scholarship to

Western Michigan University.

Will had a trio, and he allowed me to come out on Friday nights to his little gigs. I would travel to wherever they were and he paid me fifty dollars each time I performed. That was my first paid job. I was only fifteen years old then and a sophomore in high school. I continued doing this gig until I graduated from Paw Paw High School in 1956.

Even though I now had a paid gig, I kept refusing to let people limit me. So even though I wasn't getting encouragement, I would try out for all kinds of things at school. I could not afford to take music lessons or rent an instrument to be in the marching band, so I couldn't join the band. Back then, there was a letter squad at Paw Paw High School. Six young women wore letter sweaters and pleated skirts like the cheerleaders. They walked behind the baton twirlers and in front of the band. So I decided that since I didn't have to have an instrument, the letter squad was the right fit for me.

When I tried out for the letter squad, the most ridiculous thing happened to me. A white band director told me I could not march good enough to march in front of the band. Now you tell a black child whose father is a tap dancer and has been dancing since she was three years old that she didn't have enough rhythm to walk in front of a band? As it turns out, they just didn't want somebody black fronting their band. Okay. That's what that was and again it was really wrong. However, that didn't stop me from continuing to try out for things. I couldn't afford baton lessons, so I twirled a broomstick. I taught myself to twirl on a broomstick, but it didn't matter to them. Then I tried out for cheerleading. I couldn't get anybody to cheer with me, so I tried out alone. You have no idea how ridiculous it looks for somebody to cheer alone, but I did it. Well that didn't work out for me either.

Fast forward to *Sesame Street*. I had been on the show for five years when the town council called and asked me if I could be the Grand Marshal for the Grape Festival Parade—that was a big parade back in Paw Paw. I rode in a Chevy Impala convertible in front of that very band that wouldn't let me march in front of it years ago. So you can come home again and rise above the hurt and pain of discrimination. I learned so much from all of those experiences and I will never forget the feelings of accomplishment and the sense of pride I had when I was the grand marshal of the parade.

My senior portrait from the Paw Paw High School, class of 1956.

Riding with my niece in the Grape Festival Parade in

Paw Paw, Michigan back in 1974.

Celebrating with my family after the Grape Festival Parade in

Paw Paw, Michigan back in 1974.

Part 2: Western Michigan University to New York

My senior portrait from Western Michigan University, 1960

After I graduated from high school, I went to Western Michigan University. Paw Paw High School at that time was a teacher training school for Western Michigan University, which primarily was a college for people studying education. In high school, we always had many student teachers in our classrooms, which made going to Western just a bit more comfortable for me.

One day during my senior year in high school, the head of the music department from Western came to see one of his student teachers conduct the choir. Luckily for me, I had a solo that day. After the concert that administrator from Western came backstage and walked up to me. I had no idea who he was. I remember exactly what he said,

"How would you like to come to Western and sing in my choir?"

And I said, "Who are you?"

It turns out that he was always on the lookout for talent and he was able to see something in me. He offered me a scholarship to Western to sing in his choir. Thinking back about it now, this chance meeting really changed my life and it opened so many doors for me. Now, it wasn't a full scholarship and there was no way I could have gone to college without a full ride. So I applied for every kind of scholarship there was. In the end I actually had more than one scholarship. I had to work as well to be able to afford to pay for everything. I had a job as the librarian for the choir. It was a work-study position where they basically paid part of your tuition in exchange for work. Working as the librarian gave me the opportunity to take care of the sheet music for our choir. It also gave me that extra opportunity to study music, which I always loved to do.

I had several other scholarships, but the one that meant the most to me came from these two little old black ladies who were Eastern Stars. The Order of the Eastern Star is a Freemasonry-related fraternal organization open to both men and women. The two little old ladies submitted me to the Eastern Star's statewide scholarship competition. Eventually I found out that I won it. It was so incredible. They took me to Detroit when the winners were announced. Eastern Star helped pay my college tuition and bought my books when I was studying at Western. Every now and then these little old ladies would write me a letter and put five dollars in it. It was really very sweet. I was able to thank one of them who was still alive when I got on *Sesame Street*. I remember she said,

"You were the best investment we ever made."

During this time I realized that the theater department at Western was wide open. I was not stereotypically cast or not cast because of my color. You just auditioned and you got the role or you didn't. It was very interesting because Western had something called the Brown and Gold Follies, which was designed so students like me could create original work. There was always a chance for somebody to write original music, a play or a musical. I would always try out for those shows and I very often got a starring role in the Follies. Even when we did standard plays, we were not typecast or not allowed to be in the show because we were white or black. You just auditioned. It was great and a great time for me to explore my abilities as an actor.

I graduated from Western Michigan University in 1960 with a degree in education. Times were changing and I was in Michigan, so I wanted to move to Detroit and be part of the Motown sound. Even though all the slots for The Supremes were taken, I still wanted to be one of them. I didn't care, I was motivated and I knew that going back home to the farm wasn't an option. There just wasn't anything happening in show business on the farm. I was determined to never work on a farm again, even though I knew my parents could have used my help. I had to follow my dream. I had to go somewhere. I couldn't afford California or New York, so I went to Detroit. The Motown sound was really something. It was sweeping the country and bringing black culture right into white homes. It was really changing things and connecting people. To me Detroit meant Berry Gordy and Motown. It was a good place to be as a musician or a singer. So I went there because it was time to **Occupy My Dream**. I was walking out my dream.

I wanted to get a teaching job so that I could pay my own bills and work on being in the entertainment business. I had met a young woman from Michigan State and she told me to come to her school and sign up to be a sub. I decided to go to the sub office and sign up to work in the Detroit school system. But, the sub office always slows everything down. You have to wait in your house for the sub office or someone from the board to call you and tell you where to go each day.

Detroit is a far-flung town and if you don't have a car, it's really difficult to negotiate getting from your house to whatever school you needed to go to. The secret was to go to a school where the teachers assigned there didn't even want to come, present yourself and say you'll be a floater. Then you could show up there everyday and they'll just put you wherever they need you. There is always going to be somebody having a mental health day who just doesn't show up. That's what I did. I became a permanent sub in one school instead of waiting for assignments each day from the district sub office. It was an interesting school because it was pretty tough, but I liked it. One day, I was sitting in the sub office and I saw Mrs. Gordon, a teacher in that school, going by on a gurney with one of those little straight jackets on. The authorities had come and taken her out of her classroom because she had a major breakdown during class. As she was going past the sub office, the phone was ringing. It was the main office and they said,

"Loretta, we have good news for you. We have a permanent class for you."

It was the class that just drove that teacher crazy and they're putting me in there. I thought to myself, oh my God is this good news?

I went into that classroom shaking. I soon realized the thing that made this assignment interesting was that the class was filled with throwaway kids. Their classroom was an old book closet. They were in a metal room and they had all been basically kicked out of other classes and really didn't want to be in school at all. They were wild and behaved so poorly that it was impossible to get any real work done.

They rejected learning and had driven their last teacher crazy. I was so determined and I knew they couldn't make me run away. The only place I had to go was back to the farm. This group and I were a match made in heaven because they needed me and I needed them. I just hung in there with them. It took me many months to finally get them to allow me to teach them during school hours. I had them for homeroom, social studies and English. No one wanted these kids, so whoever had them for homeroom had to keep them until lunch. They were also back with me for homeroom at the end of the day.

I was still working on singing at night, so I refused to give up all of my high notes in the classroom screaming at kids. So I wouldn't raise my voice. They thought I couldn't talk and that I was afraid of them. But that wasn't the case. I just wasn't going to lose my high notes in there with those kids. So one day, it just dawned on me that when they started cutting up, I would sit down. Then I said,

"I'm not going to cheat you out of your education, so you're going to decide whether you are going to get your lesson during this class period or after school."

They didn't believe me. I would take a piece of chalk and I'd make a mark on the board and sit down. The class was always doing the boogaloo and just fooling around. I'd see this behavior and then I'd get up and I'd make a mark on the board. It took this group a really long time to figure out what those marks meant. Then they finally realized that every mark was ten minutes after school. When the board was filled up, that was their class time.

In my particular classroom, one whole side of the room was made of glass. It was all windows and I began to notice the craziest thing happening outside my windows. The kids who were free to go at the end of the day would stay out in the yard making fun of my kids through the window. Finally, one day I said to my class,

"You know how stupid they are?"

And they said, "What are you talking about? We're in here and they're free."

I said, "Yes, but they're here too. They could go home but they're so dumb they're staying after school to mess with you."

My class started laughing, and that was the turning point. Around April, they started letting me teach them during the class time. I loved teaching, but Detroit wasn't working out for me exactly the way I had thought it would. I thought that if I moved there that in no time I would be on a Motown record and be a recording artist.

Detroit at that time had a lot of music going on. There were a lot of clubs to sing in. If you made friends with musicians and they knew you could sing, sometimes they would let you sit in. It was a great time for me to really work on my singing. I had many opportunities to sing in clubs where I thought I'd get noticed. However, it actually took the whole year to get my first big audition. The opportunities just weren't there for me in Detroit.

That opportunity came one night in 1960 when I sang in a club and Mary Wells' road manager heard me. He said he really liked me and because of that performance I got an audition with Berry Gordy. The day that I actually went for the audition, I was already moving to New York. My roommate was sitting in the rental car in front of Hitsville U.S.A. She was sitting with all of our belongings and I could see her from the window. We were driving to New York that day to start over. We had given up the apartment and we both quit our jobs. There was no point in staying in Detroit. I knew I had to move to New York if I was ever going to make it as a singer or an actor. Things were just moving too slowly for me, I was ready to **Occupy My Dream** and I didn't feel like my dreams would ever come true in Detroit.

It turns out that Berry Gordy actually played my audition. People don't realize he is really a musician. He and Smokey Robinson wrote most of the early hits. They don't think of him as anything but a businessman, but he is really a songwriter. At that time, I wanted to be a jazz singer. I'll never forget what he said to me,

"You sing very well, but we're not going to have a jazz label for a long time. But I would give you a job here. You could work here.

This is like a family. We all work in production and you could probably sing background for the acts. You could work here."

Although that sounds like a great opportunity, it just wasn't for me. I didn't want to compromise my dream. It wasn't what I wanted to do. I had just finally gotten up enough courage to go to New York and leave Michigan for the first time in my adult life. Detroit was always going to be interim for me. I really wanted to go to New York, but didn't have the courage. I'm from a small town, so I cut my teeth on a bigger town. Detroit is metropolitan but not cosmopolitan. Detroit's personality is very different than Chicago's, because Chicago is more like a big city. Detroit has always been called a "country town." For me, I think it felt safer to go from my campus to Detroit. I had a lot of friends from Detroit who went to school with me, so it was kind of comfortable. I didn't know anyone in New York except my roommate from college. But I knew it was the right place for me. We moved to Detroit and then, once we felt like we were ready, we moved on to New York.

Years later, I met Martha Reeves of Martha and the Vandellas and I told her my Motown story. She said,

"Yes, he was right. You could have worked there doing something other than singing." She also said, "I worked there five years before I got my session for "Dancing in the Street.""

She named all the records that she sang background for and ran the switchboard on. I never wanted to just wait there for my chance to sing at some point in the future. I already had a college degree and I knew I could do much more. God spared me from running the switchboard at Motown Records because he gave me the courage to believe in myself and move to New York. Today, I still thank him for that. Many times in the early years of living in New York, I thought I made a mistake when nothing was happening in my career. I thought that I could be teaching in a school in Detroit and working at Motown. In my head, that felt closer to my dream than the South Bronx did, which was where I ended up teaching when we first arrived in New York City.

Eventually, in 1961 I got a job in an all-boys vocational high school in Yonkers. The New York City school system was very hard to get into, so I had to go out to the suburbs to get a full-time job. It was an interesting time for me. Since I was working at a vocational high school, it had an early dismissal. All of the students had various work-study programs to go to after school. So we actually got out of school at 1:45pm everyday. That was good for me because then I could travel back down to Manhattan and go to my acting classes or auditions. It was a good combination of teaching and being able to try to be in this business.

When I think back about it now, my first major accomplishment in the entertainment business in New York City was being selected to be in the cast of *Sweet Charity* on Broadway in 1966. Being picked by Bob Fosse to be in the cast was the first confirmation for me that

I really did have the goods to make it in New York. Bob Fosse was an American actor, dancer, musical theatre choreographer, director, screenwriter, film editor and film director. He won an unprecedented eight Tony Awards for choreography, as well as one for direction. He was nominated for an Academy Award four times, winning for his direction of *Cabaret* (beating Francis Ford Coppola for *The Godfather*). It was well known that his auditions were very tough. Primarily, he was a dancer, so you didn't just get to sing when you auditioned for him. You had to sing and move based on the notes he gave you. You really had to listen to everything that was going on.

The audition was one of the toughest I had ever done and I was very excited to be chosen to be in the cast. Except there was one problem. I was already in a show. We were performing in an old supermarket downtown. That's really off-Broadway. I mean that's off off-Broadway. It was a review called *Pins and Needles* and I had a starring role. At the time of the *Sweet Charity* audition, we were already in rehearsals and I didn't have an understudy. I just went to the *Sweet Charity* audition because I believed in practicing on auditions for parts that I really didn't want just so I could get over being afraid on stage. So, when Bob Fosse hired me and I had to turn him down, he just about had a hissy fit. He hired me to replace somebody in the chorus. It wasn't the right thing for me at that time.

When I told Bob Fosse that I had to turn it down, he said,

"Well, good luck in the supermarket!" Then he stomped out of the aisle. I'll never forget that. It was one of those moments in my life that has been etched into my memory. I am sure I was the only person he ever said that to.

A headshot from the early 1960s, New York City.

A collection of my early headshots. Taken all before there even was a place called **Sesame Street.**

Working as a runway model in New York City in the late 1960s.

Another one of my early headshots taken after I arrived in New York City in the early 1960s

However, I made the right move. I got reviewed by the *New York Times* by being a lead in the off-Broadway show. I never would have gotten that type of attention if I had taken the chorus role. That review really helped me get many other jobs in those early days in New York City. Sometimes it is very hard to not jump to what seems to be a bigger and better job at first. Once you make a commitment you need to stick to it because you should always be in the right place, at the right time with the right people.

When I was in New York, there were all of these show business magazines and little newspapers where you'd look for gigs. When they came out, they would list all of the open calls, which means you didn't have to be in the union to go in and audition. At that time, I was studying with Herbert Berghof, who was an Austrian-American actor, director and acting coach. He always said,

"The trouble with you actors is you don't show up for the audition."

We all got indignant. "Yes, we do. We go to all of them."

He said, "No, you, the core real you. You get frightened and the real you doesn't show up. Some phony caricature of who you think you are shows up. When the real you shows up, that connects with anybody. They don't have to be sophisticated to connect with the real you."

I took that to heart and I started really going to auditions, even the ones that I didn't want, so that I wouldn't be so freaked out. This way, I could be more relaxed when it was my turn to audition.

At this point, I still wanted to be a jazz singer. I don't even really remember how I heard that Cannonball Adderley, the well-known jazz alto saxophonist, was going to take a female singer on the road with him. He just recorded a new album with Nancy Wilson and I heard that he was looking for a female singer. By this time, she was too big of a star to go out with him on tour and I thought it would be the perfect gig for someone like me.

I went to that audition and a producer named Pete Long was there. He produced concerts on Randall's Island and he did concerts at the Village Gate and other venues like that. He was well known in these circles and he was someone who really understood how this part of the business worked. That was the first time I met Pete and we later fell in love. I didn't end up going out on the road with Cannonball, but I got Pete out of that audition which was so much better.

Pete encouraged me. He told me that he thought I could sing well and that I needed to do some more things in terms of acting. He also sent me to Diahann Carroll's hairdresser. I needed a new look. He really was good about grooming me for the next level. For whatever reason, I really believed him and took his advice. Sometimes, people are trying to help you and you just think it's criticism so you don't take the advice. But I took his advice and I attempted to do the things he suggested because I really wanted to **Occupy My Dream.**

By that time, Pete was working for the Apollo Theater as a manager, so I was around a lot of people in this business who were doing very well. Well, once we had broken up and I was already on *Sesame Street*, I kept hearing this story,

"You're really funny. You were so quiet when you were married to Pete."

Well, I was so out of my depth then. I mean these people were already really working in this business. I met Flip Wilson and Bill Cosby when they were opening for Pete's acts at the Village Gate. They were young in this business, but already had accomplished so much. One night, Richard Pryor was sitting on a chair backwards hanging out with me. They were all ascending like that and I was still teaching school, so what was I going to say? I had nothing to say. I just sat there with these big eyes just looking around at everything that was going on. I was just glad that somebody invited me and didn't say something like, "She can't come in here!"

Pete was somebody that was going to help you if you could stand the heat. Pete Long was not the kind of guy who was going to be your best friend. He was a coach and anybody who has played sports knows that a coach might kick you in the butt and forget they still have their cleats on. Sometimes, even getting a kick in the butt if you are headed in the right direction can advance you.

I think Pete Long served me to toughen me up. You can't come out of every audition with your feelings so hurt that you can't get your head in the game enough to go to one the next day. He didn't allow anyone to do that. Tough love. That's what it was but we didn't have a name for it then. It was just Pete Long. He also didn't suffer excuses well. You just didn't make excuses. You could do it or get out of the way because there was always someone waiting in line to be there next. His famous word when he was auditioning the kids for an ensemble of young singers from Harlem called Listen My Brother was "Next!" He made Simon Cowell look like Mary Poppins. However, he did get you ready for the real world. He was just doing what they do when you audition on Broadway.

You can't stand up there crying or go back in the wings and cry if you have a bad audition. I was once on an audition that was so brutal that I asked for the directions to the ladies room and they directed me through a door that put me on a fire escape. I accidently walked out and the door locked behind me. I had to climb down the fire escape and once I reached the street I was all dirty. I had to walk back in through the front door of the building covered in dirt. I finally found the ladies room and washed my hands and came back in the stage door to continue to audition. Now that's brutal boy.

Pete was a real mentor to me and he had a skill set that made what he told you valuable. He had done it all and he was a great producer. He liked creative people but he didn't like you making excuses if things didn't work out. He didn't like you crying and never wanted to see you express emotions about what happened on an audition. He always would say,

"Toughen up. Keep going."

I watched him really help the kids who would allow him to help them. He would let them come into the basement of the Apollo Theater and rehearse for all different kinds of shows and auditions. For many people he was a really great teacher and advisor.

I actually stopped teaching full-time when I married Pete. I taught from '61 to '65 at Saunders Trade and Tech in Yonkers. People who I worked with then tell me that the other teachers had a pool, since it seemed to them that I got married so suddenly, that I was pregnant. I wasn't pregnant. I said "you guys should have given me the money" and they laughed. That's when I decided to just go back to subbing and I knew I was taking a big risk. However, I used the same rule of thumb. Go pick a school where the teachers don't even want to be there and then you can write your own hours. When I wanted to teach, I taught. When I had an audition or something, I didn't have to ask anyone's permission to miss a day of school.

I picked a rough junior high school in the Bronx, so I didn't have

any problems just showing up. One day, I was getting off the bus, and the secretary was running down the street saying,

"Loretta ! Loretta! Hurry up! Hurry up!"

They wanted me. Once again, it worked out just perfectly.

On stage at the Apollo Theater, New York City, 1968.

I got an audition to go to Australia in 1967 to sing in nightclubs all over the country. I believe that in everything you do, you do hit your stride. I got the audition and quickly landed the gig. I went to Australia for six weeks. When I came back, I landed an off-Broadway summer stock gig. It was a star package and we were performing *Guys and Dolls* with Betty Grable. We also performed with Molly Picon in a production of *Milk and Honey*. It was a ton of work but also a great experience.

With Molly Picon, summer 1967.

During that time I auditioned for a television show called *Soul!* *Soul!* was the first all-black variety show television program produced at WNET, the PBS station in New York City. It was like a precursor to *Soul Train*. Before this, there never had been another show like this on television. Ellis Haizlip was an African American theater and television producer. He helped many artists progress in their careers, including actress Anna Maria Horsford and singers

Nicholas Ashford and Valerie Simpson. He served as the executive producer of the Public Broadcasting Service television program *Soul!* from 1967 to 1973. He really had a great vision for what this show could be. Pete Long got me the audition because the producers of *Soul!* wanted to use the Apollo Theater band to be the house band for the show. They came to Pete to negotiate that deal. I think I was part of a package deal. I'm not too proud to say I think that he said,

"Well, if you want the acts from the Apollo to come to your show and you want Reuben Phillips' band, you've got to take my wife too."

I think I was just part of the package. Someone else can only get you the audition, but you have to get and keep the job. It wasn't a slam-dunk at all. It was a job that was all hosting. I was auditioning to be a co-host and they rolled taped on my audition. They wanted to see how I worked with the other co-host. Before this audition, my television experience had been limited and up to that point I had only done a few commercials. I had never been in a television studio before and I remember being very nervous and excited. Hosting a show was very different than what I had done before. This was a very new experience for me. I knew this would be a great career opportunity and it would give me a new level of exposure. I really wanted to land this gig because it was going to be a new avenue for black entertainers to reach the New York viewing audience. I wanted to be a part of it. The interesting thing is that people forget that in 1968, even though a black act was a big hit in the black community, most of those acts weren't going to be seen on *The Ed Sullivan Show*. *Soul!* was a place where black record acts could really be on TV. During that time, they called it "tour support." The record companies had a vested interest in seeing them come on these kind of shows. That made me excited for who I might meet if I were to be cast as a host for the show. Some time passed and the show got the official green light, and I got the call that I was going to be one of the hosts for *Soul!* I was so happy and anxious and I really didn't know what to expect. The first episode premiered on WNET Channel Thirteen in New York City on September 12, 1968. It was my first appearance on television as a host. I co-hosted the first show with Alvin Poussaint, the well-known Harvard professor and psychiatrist. The guests on that first episode were Barbara Acklin, Patti LaBelle and the Bluebelles, Novella Nelson, Billy Taylor, The Vibrations & Pearl Williams Jones and Irwin C. Watson. I couldn't believe it. I was on television with some very well-known acts and it was so overwhelming. I was **Occupying My Dream**. This was a major step in the right direction. I hosted a number of episodes in 1968, but it wasn't like I could quit my day job as a substitute teacher. The gig didn't pay much and it was a far cry from a full-time job.

At the time, being on television made it funny for me teaching as a sub at the junior high school. *Soul!* was on the air on Sunday nights in New York City. But then on Monday morning, I would be back in the Bronx on 139th Street and Willis Avenue. Other teachers and some of the students started to recognize me as someone who was on television. There was this one little boy who was making money off me and I even didn't realize it. He wasn't in any of my classes but he was always standing in front of the sub office to follow me wherever I was going. He somehow knew that I was a floater. He always had two or three kids in tow and he'd say,

"Okay. You be the one to play on that movie *Soul!?*"

Well, I'm an English teacher, so I started correcting his grammar.

"No, not 'you be the one.' Am I the one? And it's not a movie. It's television."

1968: **SOUL!** *director Ivan Cury, executive producer Kit Lukas, host Loretta Long, and host Harold Haizlip (Ellis' brother) (image courtesy Christopher Lukas)*

Then he said, "Yeah, yeah, yeah, but you be the one, right?"

I said, "Yes."

He turned to the kids and said,

"Okay. Give me my quarter."

He was betting the kids that it couldn't be me because if I was on TV, there is no way in the world I would be in his school on Monday. He knew it was me and no one else would believe it. So he bet them and won.

I said, "Wait a minute. Are you making money off me? You have to at least buy me lunch." His response was,

"Huh huh huh. You be the one to play on that movie."

Soul! was my first television program and it was important to me. It was terrifying. The red light would go on the camera and it was like it sucked my brain out. I would sit there on camera and I would be so nervous. I had to do the tease and it was live.

"Hi. I'm Loretta Long. Stay tuned for *Soul!*" In the rehearsal, I'd go, "Hi. I'm…Cut."

The director would say, "Do you need a cue card for your name?"

They weren't really very nice to me. You have to remember, I had never been in a television studio before and I had no television training. Very few people did at the time. I always have to thank Ellis Haizlip because he gave me a chance to at least learn a little bit about being on camera—there was no place for me to study television. He gave me my first opportunity to do television and to this day I am still grateful.

As an actor, I think it was better not knowing what I was doing because I happen to think none of us knew what we were doing. PBS was new. Maybe the cameramen really knew how to run their cameras, but the directors didn't know what to do either. Previously, they all worked on soap operas, so they would lock the camera down in a fixed position. There was no creativity really. They just pointed the camera at you and you talked. It was up to you to make the interviews interesting. I don't know where I could have gone to learn that, except on camera. *Soul!* ran for a long time but I only stayed on *Soul!* until I got the audition for *Sesame Street.* I spent all of 1968 with *Soul!*, but by 1969 I was working on the pilot episodes of *Sesame Street.* If it wasn't for *Soul!*, I never would have even know about the auditions for *Sesame Street.*

Hosting **Soul!** *in 1968 at WNET, New York.*

Part 3: *Sesame Street*

A promotional shot from Season 1 of **Sesame Street.**

Working with Matt Robinson during Season 1 of Sesame Street.

Standing in Lincoln Center outside of the CTW Office in 1970.

I think the reason why she was chosen was because of her personality that projected through, and I think that continues. There is a joy in her. There are smiles in her. When you start going out and you start doing research with children, Loretta is going to be smiling. There is going to be a warmth about her. There is going to be a smile. I think that love translates for the kids. I think that that has to do with her own personality. There were a lot of people who didn't have that, it wasn't at their core. But if you see her, you will see a smile. That smile breaks down real barriers in terms of attention. From a research point of view, it's that joyful, loving spirit that gets projected and the children respond to it. That was from the beginning of Sesame Street *and it still remains.*

Dr. Valaria Lovelace, Director of Research,

Sesame Street *1982-1996*

I'm a woman of faith so I really believe in the idea that you have to be in the right place at the right time, doing the right thing with the right people for the right reasons. I was working for PBS already. As most people know, *Sesame Street* is a PBS show. Charlie Rosen, who was a friend of my husband, was a set decorator for *Soul!* One day, while we were shooting an episode of *Soul!*, every time the director would say cut, you would hear the sound like a nail gun, "dzz, dzz." The sound would be coming from Charlie Rosen working on something over behind a screen. You couldn't really see him or what he was actually working on.

I like to say I have intellectual curiosity. My friends say I'm just nosy. I was sneaking around to see what was going on. It turns out that the sound was coming from Charlie building this house. What I also saw was that there was a yard, a swing and these two other buildings. I didn't know it at the time, but he was making a model for the original *Sesame Street* set. They would send the model to a set shop to have it built. He was making the model of what would become the iconic *Sesame Street* set and I didn't even realize how important what I was witnessing would turn out to be. He had three-year-old twins. I thought he was making something for his boys. He said,

"Oh no. There's going to be this new children's show. Each of us are just contributing what we know how to do. I was in school with Jon Stone and he is writing the scripts. Jon knows Jim Henson, so Jim's building puppets."

It was a very Stephen Spielberg and George Lucas kind of thing. They all just did what they did and just put it in the pot for Joan Cooney, who was really the mastermind of *Sesame Street*.

Then Charlie said,

"You're a teacher, right?"

Of course, I went into my …

"Oh no, I'm an actress who just happens to teach."

He said, "Calm down. You're a teacher, right?"

I said, "Well, I have teaching credential."

He said, "Look. It's a children's show. It's going to be educational."

Now I almost blew up my own career because me and kiddie television had nothing in common. Before *Sesame Street*, here was kiddie television,

"Now be a good Do Bee. Everybody look in the magic mirror."

Me? I said,

"Oh no, thank you."

I didn't even teach little kids in school. I was a high school teacher. I responded,

"No, thank you. I'm not doing *Romper Room*."

He said,

"Now wait a minute. Don't say no so fast because this is going to be different than any children's television you've ever seen before."

Well, remember that thing I said before about how I went to every audition? I even went to an audition where it was supposed to be all guys, and I kept saying,

"I can cut my hair. I can be a guy." They said, "Get out."

That kicked in. Then I remember saying,

"Well, I might as well go to the audition."

Charlie Rosen went to his grave with this secret. I could never get him to tell me that he knew that I was supposed to be able to play a guitar for the *Sesame Street* audition. I get to the audition and I'm the only one without a guitar. They wanted a Joan Baez folk acoustic guitar player. I strolled in there, big hair, short skirt looking like Angela Davis. I was so not what they were looking for. By the time I arrived at the audition, I was so determined and I was not going to let anyone run me off. I knew that it just had to be my job, even if I wasn't what they thought they wanted.

When you show up some place and people don't expect you, they rush to the door and say things like,

"Can I help you?"

I said, "Yes. I'm here for the audition for the children's show." And they said,

"Where's your guitar?"

I said, "Excuse me?"

They said, "Everybody here plays a guitar, but you, where is your guitar?"

My fingernails were long and red. I just had them done for the audition.

I said, "I don't play the guitar."

They said, "Okay. Then stand over there."

Now, these are people I know now and they claim they said this nicely. They didn't say it nicely. It was a very stern,

"Stand over there."

I tell kids all the time that this was another defining moment in my life. That's because I could have stood in the corner like I did, or I could have gotten all huffy and puffy and gone back to the Bronx to my school. I decided to stay. The longer I stayed there, the more determined I got to sing for somebody, even if it was a janitor. I had already blown my cab fare to keep my afro kind of together. I had spent $15 on cab fare and, back then, that was a ton of money. No matter what, I was going to sing for somebody.

So I stood over in the corner and the casting team got up like they were ready to leave. I quickly said,

"Excuse me." I was still trying to be nice. "Could I talk to the piano player?"

I had my show tunes, big hair and my short skirt. They said,

"We didn't hire a piano player. Everybody here plays a guitar but you."

I said, "But I came to sing."

They said, "Okay, so sing." Then they sat back down.

I laid my little music down, and here is exactly what my audition for *Sesame Street* turned out to be. I clapped my hands, stomped my foot and then sang…

"I'm a little teapot short and stout. Here is my handle. Here is my spout."

I looked right at the camera because I'd been doing commercials for *Soul!* and I knew eye contact with the audience for television was so important. So I focused my eyes on the lens of the camera, visualizing a group of children looking back at me. Then, I invited the children in the audience to sing with me. I stopped singing and I said this directly to the kids who would be in the audience,

"You know this song. Stand up and sing with me."

Then I just continued to sing the rest of the song.

I heard that they were taking the tapes of the auditions and playing them for children. I knew I had to connect with them just like a teacher connects with students in the classroom. Well it worked.

When I stopped and told them to stand up and sing, the producers told me that the kids watching the videotape of my audition stood up and sang. This was a totally new concept at the time. For the show's producers, that was their indication that if we invited children to participate in what we were doing on camera, they would. I have some kids who were in a Harlem classroom that day to thank for a career. I wish I could find them now and give each of them a great big hug.

They hired me for five days of work during the week of July 9th, 1969. We shot the pilot shows Monday through Friday of that week. When we did the first set of pilot shows for *Sesame Street*, I was frightened, totally terrified. I was so frightened that I thought I would forget my lines or mess something up.

I thought they would replace me for sure. That's all I could think about. I kept asking myself things like, can I do this? I didn't know how to do this. I was just so nervous. I was one of those kind of people. It comes from being a minority child where you don't want to embarrass your race. To have to be good for your whole race, that's kind of a heavy-duty gig for a seven year old, but that's how I felt all through school. I had to really be good at it or I wouldn't try it. So to be thrown into the deep end of the pool and know you don't swim too well, that's all I could remember. It wasn't jubilation. It was more fear than anything else.

When I think back about all of this now, the first thing that I really remember is thinking how one phone call can really change your life. I never expected to still be doing this forty-six years later. At that time for me, just to be hired for a week's worth of work in this business, doing something new for that matter, was so thrilling. I don't remember even sleeping during that period. I was just wired.

A new experience like this usually is mostly filled with excitement, but you're also so scared at the same time. During that week, it seemed like all I did was really just calm myself down. Then I would get up the courage to just go to the studio and I sat and observed what was going on. Watching Jim Henson and Frank Oz operate Ernie and Bert for the first time, meeting Will Lee and Bob McGrath and observing Jon Stone directing are memories I'll never forget. It was a truly amazing week and I really enjoyed the work. I was hopeful that I would get hired for more shows.

I first became aware of Loretta Long when Jon Stone showed me a tape of her audition. She was reading dialogue from the script and he said,

"And she can sing too."

I said, "Hire her."

Then he said, "She's a teacher too."

And I said, "Don't wait, just get her." That was when I first became aware of her and she has been on the show even since.

Joan Ganz Cooney, Co-Creator of **Sesame Street**

With Joan Ganz Cooney in New York City, December 2014.

My cousins are wheat farmers out in Kansas and they use these big combines on their farm. They are the farmers with the tractors so tall that you have to climb up the ladder to get on them. When you get out in front of those bad boys, you're out of their sight. You have to be so careful or they'll run over you. I took that good advice to just come and be part of the environment and just look around and see what was going on. I knew I had to try to not make a fool out of myself or I'd just get run over. So I really worked hard to just watch the other actors on set and take away whatever I could from those who had more experience than I did.

Thank God I had enough experience from being on *Soul!* that at least I could say my name on camera. When the red light went on, I wasn't totally paralyzed. I had a little acclimation to a TV studio. But boy, when you talk about when Jim Henson and his merry men—that's what I always called Jim and the puppeteers—arrived on set, it was like watching a television genius at work. The first time I saw them, I had never seen white guys look the way they looked before.

Now this was the 60s, so everybody had a lot of hair. Jim had this chestnut brown shoulder length hair and this very benevolent look on his face. He was a very calm guy. His wife, Jane, made his clothes, so everything was buckskin lashed together. They all had handmade sandals from the Village. I recognized them because, back then, everybody you knew tried to save up their money and went to the same sandal maker as they did. They drew your foot and made your custom-made sandals. It was a hip thing at that time.

I got tickled because they walked like a V. Jim would lead and all the puppeteers would fall in behind him like a flock of geese. They came walking through the set and I said,

"Who is that?"

Then someone said with this great voice,

"Oh, that's Jim Henson."

I was in awe. I just waited around for Henson's people to talk to me. I didn't talk to anyone who didn't talk to me first.

Jim Henson was very, very nice. I don't think there could be a nicer person to work with. When you watched him work, he was so serious. He wasn't funny until he had that puppet on his hand. And we all know how amazing it was to see him working with the Muppets on screen. He made the *Sesame Street* characters come to life like no one else could have ever done. But backstage, he was very quiet.

It was so interesting and amazing when Jim Henson, Frank Oz and the team would work. After each take, all of the actors and crew would wait for Jim to stand up from behind the puppet set. He'd say either,

"Moving on."

Or he'd say, "We can do better!"

Then he would simply just disappear again. That was it and it was his call. No one in the control room said anything to him. They waited for him. His presence on set coupled with his vast television experience had a powerful effect on everyone. He wasn't overbearing, but everyone on set knew when he was there.

I had no idea that working television was going to be as hard as it was. It's very time-consuming. We laughed because you get into a limbo. You come to work in the dark, and you leave the studio in the dark. It's like collapsed time. It's like you're in some kind of vacuum and your reality is that studio. When your reality has Muppets and a set that looks like a typical inner city street but it's all actually inside a building, that's kind of bizarre. As an actor, it really was kind of strange to get your head around. But once we all did, I think that's where the magic of *Sesame Street* comes from.

We did five pilot shows because everyone involved felt that there was no way to show a pilot of *Sesame Street* in an hour or two. The basis of the show was teaching like you taught in a classroom. You introduced a concept and then, day after day, you worked on it with your class. So we treated our audience like they were sitting in a classroom. Our writers actually would write to a syllabus, just like a teacher would use to plan out a lesson. It's really a difficult show to write for because the producers would say,

"Okay. Scott, you're going to write Monday's show. You're going to have to teach the concept of 'near and far.' You have to use Gordon, Susan, Grover, Big Bird and Oscar. Oh, and you have to make it funny."

Then after you labor over your little script, your little baby, you have to hand it to the research department. The educational researchers are there to make sure you haven't muddied the educational concept and your show does not get on until they sign off on it. Most comedy writers, they'd slit their throats if somebody had to sign off on their being funny. But our show is very unique because you have the production people and then you have the educators sitting right behind them in the same control room. We're not allowed to muddy any educational concept for the sake of a laugh.

After we wrapped up the five pilot episodes, we didn't know what was going to happen. We had to wait and see if someone was going to buy it. Eventually, we were told that we had been bought for thirteen episodes, which was a standard season back then. It was so exciting. It was something new and I was a part of it. I was elated when I found out that I was going to be part of the cast. Since then, the actors' contracts, even mine, have been set up for one season at a time. So when you fast forward to today and think about this for a minute, it's pretty amazing. Bob McGrath and I are the only two remaining cast members who were with *Sesame Street* since the five pilot episodes. The two of us have been given contracts, one season at a time, for all forty-six years. I think that's a pretty amazing thing for television actors and I am pretty sure we are the only ones with that kind of longevity with one specific show.

I wasn't really paid much for working on the pilot episodes. I was just happy to be working and to be on television. Thank God Harold Orenstein entered my life. He was my first lawyer and he was the man who set up a publishing company for Gordon Lightfoot and Paul Simon. His main thing was music publishing, but he took me on as a client. He took one look at my salary and said, "Oh no, you got to do better for her than this."

So the first season was good. We got paid scale for the pilot and the rest of season one but looking back it wasn't very much. However, it was more money than I had ever made before so I was happy. Honestly, I was happy to be working anywhere other than the family farm back in Paw Paw, Michigan. I never would have ended up on *Sesame Street* if it wasn't for Charlie Rosen and Pete Long. Pete also helped a group of young black singers from Harlem called Listen My Brother get onto three of the five test shows for *Sesame Street* as well. Thinking back about it now, that was kind of incredible. It was almost like a college football coach having two of his players drafted to play on the same NFL team.

Listen My Brother was an ensemble of young men and women that included Luther Vandross. One of Pete's goals for the group was to help the members get scholarships to go to college. I would check their report cards at the end of each term and Pete and I encouraged the group to continue their education beyond high school. We even helped Luther Vandross earn a scholarship to my alma mater Western Michigan University, although he left after one year to focus more on his professional career.

Pete would rehearse the group in the basement of the Apollo Theater and often booked them as opening acts for some of the big names that would come through the Apollo in the late 1960s and early 1970s. In early July of 1969, when production began on the test shows for *Sesame Street*, Pete arranged to have Listen My Brother perform their version of the "Alphabet Song" in the television studio where we were shooting the show. It was decided later that this segment would be used in the very first test show of *Sesame Street*. The group tested well and was invited back to the show. This time they appeared again but the songs they sang were shot on the street set.

The songs they sang appeared on a number of episodes beginning in 1970 and appeared as inserts for many years to come in many different episodes of *Sesame Street*. I recently had the chance to speak to two members of Listen My Brother, Fonzi Thornton and Bruce Wallace. I asked them to reflect on their appearances on *Sesame Street* and their experiences working with Pete Long. I wanted to include this in my book because Fonzi and Bruce are a part of my story.

Bruce Wallace, member of Listen My Brother, *reflects on being on* **Sesame Street***:*

Appearing on **Sesame Street** *was truly awesome because it actually spearheaded my career in music. It was unimaginable that we would ever be on TV. The beautiful thing about it was, when it first came on, we were sitting at the screen with bated breath. We were all thinking that it wasn't going to come on. We sat with family, friends, and people from the neighborhood waiting and, when it finally came on, it was just awesome. Our segments were on so many times the first and the second year of the show, it was truly incredible. We had no reference as to what* **Sesame Street** *actually was or was going to be. When we arrived in the studio and we actually saw the street set sitting inside a building it was amazing within itself.*

First of all, I didn't even think that I was going to be on the show. This was because Diane, one of the ladies in Listen My Brother *who was supposed to be on the show that day, didn't show up for the shoot. No one actually knew where she was. So, Pete Long asked me to go in her place because they already had the shot set for a certain number of people. So the reason that I was actually able to do that was because I used to sing with Luther Vandross and Fonzi Thornton in a different group. This was just before we got to* Listen My Brother. *So when I used to go to the rehearsals, I actually never went to* Listen My Brother *as a singer, I actually*

admired Pete Long and I used to sit and just watch the rehearsals.
Really, I wanted to do what Pete did because he was in charge. I
wanted to be Pete Long, I really did. I really wanted to be Pete
Long, but that particular day, they didn't let me be Pete Long.
They told me I had to stand in for Diane and luckily I knew all
the songs. I actually knew all her parts, just an octave lower. So
Luther and everyone else involved said,

"That'll be fine, just go ahead and sing."

So I went ahead and sang. Thinking back on what happened after
that performance, I believe it was Pete and Loretta's decision to
send me to do two other opportunities that became immediately
available after I did well on the **Sesame Street** *shoot. For the first*
one, they took me to audition for **The Electric Company.** *And on*
top of that, they sent me for the audition for the **Muppeteer**
Workshop. *I actually didn't know enough about what I was doing*
for either one of those auditions, but they believed in me. I went
and they asked me to make up different voices. I just came up
with them on the spot and did some voices for the audition. They
also put me in school to train for the summer and gave me a
stipend to teach me how to do puppets with Jim Henson. The
summer culminated when we shot a scene that they actually used
on **Sesame Street.** *I was in the back and there were like eight of*
us and we were all performing Kermit on the stage. So when it

finally came on TV, I'm on as a puppet and everybody said,

"Well, which one are you?"

Because everybody looked exactly the same, all I could say was...
"I'm the one in the back."

I didn't pursue anything else with **Sesame Street** *after that. And once Listen My Brother broke up, I ended up working with Teddy Pendergrass doing his choreography and I stayed on with him for a year. That's when Luther Vandross's career took off. I stayed on the road as his choreographer. Then I later learned how to do lighting. All of this stems from being on* **Sesame Street** *and seeing all the things that were going on and all the pieces involved in the background. I always wanted to be in the background. So I stayed on the road with Luther for ten years.*

Appearing on **Sesame Street**—*it just seemed like something that was beyond my wildest dreams. I just never imagined that anything like that would ever occur. Here's the funniest thing: When we appeared on the show they had me sing this song called, "Children Are Beautiful."*

The funny thing about "Children Are Beautiful" was that they told me that now I had to sing a solo line about children from all over the world being beautiful. My line was "whether from Germany." When I got on the stage, we were sitting on something that looks like a fire escape. When it got to be the time for me to sing "whether from Germany," I couldn't do it.

I just said, "Whether from Germany," instead of singing it. And the song just went on, I was just reciting it. Then everyone said,

"Why didn't you sing the part?"

The reason I didn't sing it was because I thought that they were going to say that there was a mistake and have us do the number again. But, they kept it in and kept it moving. I was expecting a second take and third take. Well it didn't happen and I found out later that they rarely redid anything.

Actually the appearance on **Sesame Street** *gave me the wherewithal to continue to dream. That's it. Period. It made me realize that anything was possible. For this to happen to me out of the clear blue sky was amazing to me. To go from the basement at the Apollo Theater to being on a national syndicated television show and to see my face on the screen over and over and over again, at that point, I realized that anything was possible.*

Pete Long was like my idol. He really was because I really did not understand that there were people that actually directed the performers and told them what to do. I just thought people got on the stage and they did whatever they did. But when I sat with Pete at first and Pete said,

"I'm going to make you a stage manager. What you do is you sit next to me and you keep notes."

So I sat next to him and I kept notes. I also kept people from being late. I used to be like a timekeeper. Later on, Pete told me that this was one of the things that helped me get so many jobs. Early on, I realized that you needed to be on time to stay employed in this business. I kept that philosophy during my whole career and through my whole life. To be on time has always been important to me. A lot of times, being on time makes all the difference in the world.

Later on in my career when I was on the road with Luther Vandross, Pete actually came to the Universal Amphitheater to see the show. Pete came backstage and he said,

"Well, who actually directed and choreographed the show?"

Luther said,

"Bruce did."

Pete said,

"Bruce did?"

Luther said, "Yes."

Pete said,

"That was the greatest show that I have ever seen."

That compliment stuck with me. It meant a lot to me that after all those years he would come back and see what we were doing. I'll never forget that and the feelings I had when I realized how proud he was of me.

Fonzi Thornton, member of Listen My Brother, reflects on being on **Sesame Street***:*

Listen My Brother was the beginning of my professional training as a performer and **Sesame Street** *was my very first TV appearance. Since then I've had a very long professional career as a solo singer, a stage performer, a session vocalist, a songwriter and producer. I appeared on* **Sesame Street** *with Listen My Brother the second year that we performed on the show. The group included myself, my best friend Luther Vandross, Robin Clark and Elaine Clark. The group choreographer Bruce Wallace stood in a for a girl named Diane Sumler. Diane was one of the regular members of the group, but she had taken sick the morning of the show and didn't make it to the taping.*

I knew Luther Vandross and Bruce because Luther had put together a group that we were all in. I lived in the Johnson Project in Harlem and Luther's sister Anne lived in a building across the street. Luther's vocal group that he had put together in the neighborhood was called the Shades of Jade. My girlfriend and I went over to join that group and we appeared in the Apollo Theater amateur night twice with them. We came in second place both times.

Some time passed and Luther told me about this group, it was a musical review which was organized at the Apollo, called Listen My Brother. I thought it was a funny name. He said that they were a group of talented teens. He said most of the people were teenagers, but some of them were young adults in their early twenties. He also said it was a review and a workshop run by this guy named Peter Long who was one of the managers at the Apollo Theater. Luther told me he auditioned and had gotten in. So that explained why he had totally lost interest in our group, Shades of Jade.

I wanted to know all about this, especially because Luther told me that Listen My Brother was opening shows for some the major artists at the Apollo and were doing TV shows like the **David Frost Show.** *So I knew I really had to hear what this group was all about. I followed him to the Apollo Theater. Outside the theater, there was a doorway right next to the box office on the right hand side. It led down a long staircase into this funky rehearsal hall. In the room there was a wooden floor and around the side of the room there were benches. There were mirrors and things like that for dancers to practice with.*

So I went into this room and there were a bunch of kids sitting on the benches. In the center was this guy Pete Long. So Pete said to me,

"What are you doing here?"

I said, "Well my name is Alfonso."

He said, "Why did you come down here?"

I said, "Because my friend told me about the group."

He said, "Well what are you, a singer of something?"

I said, "Yeah, I'm a singer."

He said, "Well sing something then."

I can't really remember what I sang, but I had to sing in front of everyone. I remember that when I first opened my mouth, nothing came out. So Pete took his hands and clapped them together, like on the beat. Then he said,

"Alfonso, what is the problem?"

So then I sang and he said, "That sounds pretty good, why don't you come in tomorrow."

Listen My Brother rehearsed every evening at 7pm and we were there for several hours. It was really an amazing training ground. Tommy Johnson was a choreographer. George Stumps was the musical director – he was also the director of the Apollo House Band. On top of that we had Pete Long, who was a mentor and just a brilliant person. He taught us everything from how to stand, to microphone techniques and even simple stagecraft. He even brought amazing artists down to talk to us from the likes of Donny Hathaway to Nancy Wilson.

The biggest perk when we were in the group was when Pete arranged for us to come to the theater after school and get in to see the Apollo shows. That was part of our training—to watch professional artists do what they did. So we would go there after school and sit in the Apollo Theater all afternoon long and see acts like Nancy Wilson, Dionne Warwick, James Brown and Tommy Hunt.

Pete's main requirement was that if you're going to be in this group you had to get good grades in school. Pete's wife Loretta Long checked our report cards to make sure we were keeping our grades up. She came by from time to time to check them. She was this attractive lady with an afro. We were all sort of in awe of her because, first of all, she was Pete's wife. Secondly, we all remembered her face from being the hostess on a Channel 13 show called Soul!

Listen My Brother was a topical review during the Civil Rights Movement. Edgar Kendricks, who was part of the group, was like a genius singer and a songwriter and just a dynamo. He wrote all of these amazing songs that were the core material of the review.

Songs like "Listen My Brother," which the group got its name from. The song said, "Listen my brother to what we've got to say, we're on our way." He also wrote the song, "I'm Going to Make It."

Pete was so amazing. He was able to get all of these people together and we learned our craft by doing it. Not just by singing, but by doing choreography and doing dramatic transitions in each song. The song "I'm Going to Make It" had a dramatic piece that preceded the song being sung. A protagonist would come on stage and agitate everybody and say,

"You're not going to make it. You're not going to be nothing. You're not going to be nothing."

Each of us would have to get up and explain why we were going to make it. Then the act would go into the song and I always thought that this was a brilliant setup. Edgar Kendricks, who had written all of those songs, also wrote the songs that we performed on **Sesame Street.**

I was in the second wave of the group. The group had appeared on **Sesame Street** *the year before I joined because of Loretta's influence. Loretta had landed the job as Susan on* **Sesame Street** *and it was through her that the group had a chance to go on* **Sesame Street** *and to do some songs. One day after I had been in the group for a while, Pete said to us,*

"We're going on Sesame Street again—well this time it's going to include you."

I said, "Oh my God, I can't believe this!"

My first impression of Sesame Street came when we walked down the street to get into position to perform. When you see Sesame Street on TV, it just looks like a more enhanced version of an urban street in Harlem or Brooklyn. So when I got on the set, I was just knocked out because, being there, it was like enhanced ten times from how it looked on TV. First of all, all the colors were brilliant. Seeing all the sets, the props, the backdrops, the lights, cameras and the puppets was so amazing. It was like just magic to be in the center of all of that.

I've been on TV a lot since then doing a lot of different things but that first experience is still the most amazing. That day when we were there performing on the set doing our numbers, every time we had a little break we were trying to look around and see everything that was going on. Of course we were trying to be cool because Pete had that watchful evil eye. He made you be professional at all times.

The thing about Pete that was amazing, besides being a taskmaster and mentor and all that stuff, was that he was also very much a loving father figure for all of us. A lot of the people that were in the group didn't have fathers at home. Fortunately, I had my mother and father both at home, but Pete was such an influence and he gave tough love and we all benefited from it.

When we performed on **Sesame Street,** *we sang, "Those are the ABC's." I had a little step-out part during that song where I sang my step-out verse as I walked on the wall in front of Susan and Gordon's apartment building. We did another song called "Count to 20," where Luther, Bruce and I had a trio part where we climbed up this staircase singing. We had another song called "The Parts of the Body" where we did all this choreography. "Children are Beautiful" was the last song we did. So between the set of the songs, we were all peeking around the set. I remember, I saw Oscar's garbage can. I was sitting next to it and I opened the lid and looked into it and Oscar was in there. It was amazing.*

So ironically, after we finished the song "Count to 20," we heard this voice saying,

"What's going on around here?"

Then we all looked up and Oscar was coming up out of the garbage can. We were just all stunned because to see him in person, after having seen him on TV, just floored us. So between another set of numbers, we moved a little bit further onto the set and I peeked around again. I peered around this corner and there on the floor was this big yellow costume. It was actually Big Bird. But it was split in half and the top half was sitting on the floor. The other half was made up of the legs and it was sitting right next to it on the floor. The eyes were blank and it was just staring straight ahead and it was silent. It was sort of creepy and incredible at the same time. I wanted to touch it but I wouldn't dare to touch it because I was scared. We were there being professional and I was trying to do what we were there for.

After we finished the next number, I remember looking up and seeing this big yellow bird walking around the studio talking to different people. He was just bending down and talking to people, just engaging in conversation. I was just amazed that some inanimate creature like that could come to life and have a soul and make an impression on everybody who was there. My whole experience on **Sesame Street** *ingrained in me that I was going to absolutely be in showbiz. I was going to absolutely take off the mantle of responsibility and just keep walking forth. It was the most magical day I think I've ever had. We were like the luckiest people in the world to be there on that set.*

That second year when we were on **Sesame Street,** *the show had become such a big hit. It was just amazing that we went and looked in Mr. Hooper's store and we went behind the set of Susan and Gordon's apartment house. On TV these looked like real* buildings, but just to see the magic of the stagecraft and how things were done left me an with an exceptional impression.

The show we were on was shown a couple of times over the next couple of weeks. After that, they broke the numbers off and inserted them into different shows for the rest of the year. Then over the next year and a half they were used again. After that they would appear every now and then for many years to follow. They just used those songs that we sang as if we were guests on the show. They were teaching songs and we were young people singing these songs, so they fit into Sesame Street very well. So I saw the show many, many, many times and, in fact, we became little local celebrities. People would call my mother and say "I saw your son on Sesame Street." It was amazing. Even more recently, I've seen some of the clips because a fan uploaded some of them to YouTube. Seeing them again and looking at my face and seeing this youthful thing, seeing the gleam in my eye, and just seeing the hope I had then brought me back in time.

Pete Long taught all of us one thing that everyone who went on to have professional careers retained. It was that whenever you are standing in front of a microphone you should raise your face to look up at the third balcony, so people could look into your eyes and into your face and see your expression. I see so many young people on TV today that are wearing dark glasses and we don't know what they're doing; we don't know their expression. When I *look back at the Listen My Brother tapes I realize now that, even then, communicating with your audience was something we did. That was something that came from the training Pete gave us. It was something we owed the audience and that came from the opportunity to do it. After the* **Sesame Street** *appearance, Pete approached me and told me that there were going to be some road shows with some of the cast. He said that there was going to be some children's concerts that Loretta Long and Bob McGrath were going to do. They were going to take a show of children's concerts on the road and travel the United States and Canada. I was chosen to be one of the three background vocalists for the show. So it was my very first tour. Now mind you, I have since toured all over the world with Aretha Franklin and Luther Vandross and Roxy Music and everybody in between, but that was my first tour. I learned how to be in a professional touring company and the responsibilities that come with that. I believe that the influence of Listen My Brother and the* **Sesame Street** *appearances are what propelled Luther Vandross to take all of his amazing talent and become the great superstar that he was. So we were always proud of our involvement in the group. We always owed a major debt of gratitude to Pete and then also to Loretta Long for just getting us the chance to have a view into the professional side of the business.*

Part 4: Life on *Sesame Street*

Working on the set of Sesame Street *in the 1970s.*

Sesame Street *really was created to fill a gap and to reach out to disadvantaged children to enable them to have positive images. It enabled them to have educational support that maybe some middle-class kids already had.* Sesame Street *was really our version of Head Start.*

The target audience was minority children and we needed to have strong minority images on the show. Susan and Gordon were critical to creating a place where children could see themselves accepted and see role models that looked like them achieving things. This was all happening on the street where there was interaction, love and support between diverse people. To see that diversity of people living on the street together, that was the key.

One of the goals was creating an image where people were learning, laughing and having fun together. We wanted to show them enjoying life together. We also wanted to show that they were able to function together and work through some issues and problems together.

Susan played a critical part in that. We know that mothers are usually children's first teachers. When it comes to the person that children admire the most, we're talking about moms. She was everyone's mom on the show. There had to be a strong female role model there. If not one, many. They knew children would really understand that representation.

I think it was critical because I think that family is very important. I think having a mother and a father sends a very strong message. To see these two people ... they may not be in the same segment, they may be together, but they're managing the raising of these children. They are raising these Muppets and caring for them as well. We saw the male point of view of parenting and the female point of view of parenting and that was important.

Dr. Valaria Lovelace, Director of Research,

Sesame Street, *1982-1996*

Initially, in the test episodes that we produced and tested on television in Philadelphia before the show went on the air, Susan and Gordon weren't married. That was at the top of my list of changes for the show. My first note was Gordon and Susan must be married because we were trying to model desirable behavior for children in the audience. So we quickly married them. I said, "they're clearly kind of mommy and daddy on the street whether they're called that or not." I said, "get them married and have them be the kind of parents that the kids and the Muppets would need to have around." Loretta is still on the show partially because the show is still on. We never could have known that when we started that forty-six years later we'd still be there. Secondly, our love of tradition on the show keeps her on Sesame Street. *Lastly,* Sesame Street *is* Sesame Street, *and it's never going to change. But there's no mystery as to why she's still there—because she's good. She's beloved. On screen, we've kept our family together for all these years.*

Initially I knew I wanted four hosts because I didn't want a host to own the show the way that Captain Kangaroo owned his show. That's because if they leave, they can hold you up and there are just all kinds of things they can do. I wanted Hispanics and African Americans to be represented as the top cast members. We started out, with just African Americans. Then the Hispanic community came down on our head. There was a virtual sit-in in my office. Later on we added characters like Luis and Maria to the cast. Diversity was always important on **Sesame Street** *and it always will be.*

Joan Ganz Cooney, Co-Creator of **Sesame Street**

Working with Matt Robinson, who played Gordon for the first three season of **Sesame Street.**

During the first season, *Sesame Street* introduced the characters of Gordon and Susan, a black couple who were married. During that time there were very few positive representations of black families in any form of media, especially television. There was the NBC sitcom *Julia*, which came on television a year before *Sesame Street* did. The actress Diahann Carroll was playing a single mother. However, on most shows black children and black families were represented in a very stereotypical fashion. Almost all representations of black families showed a broken home of some kind, including *Julia*. So it was very unique that Susan and Gordon were a black married couple who owned their own house. I was thrilled to be a part of this television couple because I felt that we were breaking new ground on television. Most people point to *The Cosby Show* as the first television show to depict a non-stereotypical black family. But, *The Cosby Show* didn't have its first episode until 1984. This was 1969 and we were making a major step forward for the black family on television.

That's right, as I just mentioned, Gordon and Susan owned 1-2-3 Sesame Street. That's the very recognizable and iconic brownstone apartment building on *Sesame Street*. That has gotten kind of forgotten over the years on the show. But, not only were we a black married couple, we also owned that house. We had some strange tenants like Big Bird, Oscar the Grouch, and Ernie and Bert. But, we were landlords, which was not the typical case for black families on television.

During that time there were only four human cast members seen on screen in the street scenes. They were Mr. Hooper (Will Lee), Bob (Bob McGrath), Susan (well that's me) and Gordon (Matt Robinson). Three males and me, that was the whole human cast. There were many puppets, but male puppeteers performed most of them. This included Jim Henson, Frank Oz and of course Caroll

Spinney who portrayed Big Bird and Oscar the Grouch.

After the first season aired on television, NOW, the National Organization for Women, started monitoring the show. They did it in a very smart way. They documented that I was being marginalized as a woman. They didn't get caught up in the race issue. That wasn't their concern. All Susan ever did on the show during that first season was come to the window and want to know if someone wanted milk and cookies. I also always seemed to be dressed in an apron.

So, NOW took care of that. They came and presented a very sound argument to our show's producers that I could potentially be a wonderful role model for young girls. They ended up doing a study of the show and presented the research they had to the show's producers. The research study stated that they felt that my character was being marginalized. Honestly, I felt that same way but, at that time, I was just happy to be working. Since I was afraid that it might cost me my job, I never had the ability to say that to anyone. I was so happy that they were watching and paying attention to what was happening on screen.

After the NOW study, they had their members do a letter writing campaign to the show and to PBS stations. As I was collecting artifacts for this book I was able to find over fifty letters that NOW members had written. The letters are part of the *Sesame Street* Collection in the National Public Television Archive at the University of Maryland. Here's an except from one of the letters from the early 1970s.

*Your program Sesame Street reaches millions of children
throughout the country. Why do you persist on picturing women
as simple-minded, do nothing individuals?*

*We voiced our opposition to your portrayal last year. If you do
want children to grow up with more tolerance and understanding
of all people it is time that you extend this to women.*

Central New York NOW Chapter President

January 1, 1972

When I reflect on the NOW study, I guess I wasn't so surprised that they were angry at us. I was furious at them. I mean, I just was furious at this because I felt that these women that were on my case were upper-middle class women who did not have disadvantaged children. How dare they come at me on these issues when we were trying to do something good? What we were doing was so much bigger and important to us, than this. Now, I'm all for the women's movement and I'm very happy it exists, but I was furious at them. With all the things around to attack, we were the last thing they should have been attacking. They never gave us any credit for what we were doing. But back then, they were attacking anything they could. **Sesame Street** *was so important when it went on the air that it was a worthy target for them. We had something that people were really watching and they knew it. After I calmed down, I didn't mind that Susan was a nurse. That was fine with me. The fact that Susan and Gordon didn't have children meant she almost certainly would have had a career. We made her a nurse and I felt that was fair enough because most of those mothers in the audience are working anyway. Then we got criticized again because we were only making her a nurse. I said, "Well, what's she supposed to be? A brain surgeon?" It didn't make any sense. I finally quit fighting with them and we all moved on.*

Joan Ganz Cooney, Co-Creator of **Sesame Street**

After the letter writing campaign, the writers had Susan come to her husband and say that she wanted to go back to her career in nursing. Susan didn't ask his permission to go to work. We had a nice little chat outside of the 1-2-3 building, and I said,

"I miss nursing and I think I could do some good for the community by using my training."

Just like that, Susan went back to nursing. Now it was a dual career black family that owned their own home. For 1971, this was a very positive depiction of what black families in America were like. *Sesame Street* did this more then thirteen years before *The Cosby Show* ever aired. It was groundbreaking and, I think, for the children and families watching back then, Gordon and Susan were truly role models. Eventually, we went on tour all over the country and I really felt like an ambassador for our race. It wasn't a burden. I was very proud to do it. To go to middle America and to see lines of only white people coming to see me was truly amazing. They really connected with my portrayal of Susan and I think that helped to break down racial barriers that existed all over the country at that time.

I think one of the things that really made the show work was the ensemble cast. Bob McGrath played a music teacher on the show. His backstory was that he was from the Midwest. We wrote for the writers what our backstories were and I put a lot of my real life in it. I wrote that I was raised on a farm in the Midwest and Bob was raised on a farm in the Midwest too, so we had that in common. I think that led to us working very well together on screen. Even though I was black and he was white, the commonality of being Midwesterners was easy for children to connect to.

Will Lee, who played Mr. Hooper, he was total East Coast, Lower

East Side Jewish, total New Yorker. The intergenerational piece with Mr. Hooper was very interesting. It was amazing that they would cast a man of his age on a kid's show. He loved it. He dearly loved working on *Sesame Street*.

One day on set, he was cleaning the counter at Mr. Hooper's store, and he said,

"This is the best retirement job I could ever have dreamed of."

He said, "I'm just going to go on to heaven from here. I'm not going to be one of those little old guys in a nursing home some place scared and lonely."

He was serious. It was his birthday that day and he was telling us how happy he was for this to be his retirement job. I always loved working with him.

Caroll Spinney was so interesting because he always worked so hard. He still does. He was either in the Big Bird suit or he was in the trashcan. In the early days he was in just about every scene, either as Big Bird or Oscar. He'd always been a puppeteer. He wasn't originally one of Jim Henson's puppeteers. He didn't work on *Sam and Friends* or anything like that. He worked on many different things before coming to *Sesame Street*. He played Bozo the Clown in a local television production of the show. He also did many other local television shows in Boston and he had been a character called Mr. Lions. On that show he was dressed in a lion's suit. Because he was such a good artist, he would take somebody's name and turn it into a painting. He had a children's television background as a puppeteer. He is so talented and I was impressed with him and his hard work ethic right when I met him.

Jim Henson used to hire his people from big puppet gatherings and conventions. People would come to these events and do their act. It was like an audition. When Jim first saw Caroll Spinney, Caroll had some very elaborate set up that he had rigged up and it was all electronic. Caroll was under the table and basically his whole set up blew up. Just as things were blowing up, this hush came over the room.

"Jim Henson's here! Jim Henson's here! Jim Henson!"

As this was happening, Caroll's set up was shorting out and blowing up. It's so funny the way he tells this story. He says that he was so embarrassed he wouldn't come out from the back of the puppet stage because whatever was supposed to happen didn't happen and it blew up in front of everyone.

The next thing he knew, here's Jim Henson on all fours down there looking at him face to face and Jim was asking,

"You want to come work for me? I got what you were trying to do. You want to come and work for me?"

Obviously, Caroll said, "Okay," but he says that was the worst audition he'd ever had until Jim climbed under the table to hire him. I am so grateful that Jim hired Caroll. He's been a pleasure to work with all of these years and wonderful friend to me.

A lot of people don't realize this, but I've worked with three different Gordons on the show. The little kids think I'm burying them under the stoop. There was someone who played Gordon in the original pilot of *Sesame Street* and, for the longest time, no one seemed to know his name. In 2011, Sesame Workshop released a short video clip from the very first test pilot show that featured him. They asked the internet community to see if someone could identify him. After sometime, his family contacted Sesame Workshop and it turns out that his name was Garrett Hobart Saunders. Garrett worked primarily as a local actor in New York City and he performed in traveling theater.

They tested street scenes that featured Garrett and me, and he didn't test well. So when it was time to shoot the season one pilot the producers asked Matt Robinson, who was a producer from Philadelphia and a writer, to play Gordon. Matt was initially hired to produce and oversee filmed segments focusing on the diversity of different characters on the show. The other producers kept saying,

"We want a Matt Robinson type to play Gordon."

We got right up to taping the pilot and the producers got together and said,

"Matt, come on. You got to do this," and he really didn't want to.

He wasn't an actor and didn't want to be. For the sake of the show, he did that first season but he kept telling them,

"You all better find somebody else because I'm not doing this forever."

I think he lasted for three seasons and then he just refused to do it. By 1972, Hal Miller was playing Gordon. He appeared on the show in Season 4 and Season 5. Hal Miller eventually left the show and worked in Hollywood afterwards. And then of course there's the Gordon who's still on the show that everyone can recognize, Roscoe Orman. I still enjoy working with him today and I think he has been a true asset to the show. His portrayal of Gordon is beloved by many generations of *Sesame Street* viewers.

I think that the cast had chemistry right from the start. As soon as we began working together something interesting happened. The show was the star, not us. We were an ensemble and we were really just one of the elements. The Muppets were also one of the elements. The concept was the star. It really was. We all felt doing something this important for kids took that egomaniac actor stuff and neutralized it. We were never like that, which created a wonderful working environment that made our cast very much like a family.

What was so amazing about the whole demeanor of the cast and crew in the early days of the show is that no one thought a lot of themselves. We weren't superstars. In our first set of offices, there were four offices where you got off the elevator and that's where all the important folks sat. Co-creator Joan Cooney's office was almost directly across from the elevator and her door was always open. That meant you could always talk to her. She was accessible; you could always come and talk with her about anything.

She was interesting to me because she had everyone that she trusted in the places where she wanted them. She didn't micromanage. She thought of herself as a person who put on the red suit and went to Washington and got the money to finance the show. She was the face of the company. She didn't come down to the studio and mess with us about Big Bird or tell us to do something over. She had people that she trusted in those key positions and I think that you really didn't see Joan unless you were in some kind of firefight and couldn't solve it yourself. I admired that about her because she really cared about the show and she trusted the people that were in those key positions to do their jobs, but she was accessible. I certainly respected that and it helped the show come into its own.

We were happy once the show began to get noticed by the mainstream media because that meant another year on the air. One thing that you've got to understand is that we had to wait every year to be funded. So you didn't really bask in your last year's magazine cover because you were already hoping that the funding was going to come in for the next taping year. The funniest thing I ever heard Joan say was when they renamed the street in front of Lincoln Center 1-2-3 Sesame Street for the 40th anniversary of the show. At that ceremony, she said the funniest thing to me.

She said, "Everybody thinks that the 40th season is the miraculous season. Season two was a miraculous one because we didn't know we were going to be funded."

Once we made it to the second season of the show, I still didn't even realize we were a hit. I didn't give up my sub license for ten years after the show started. No, no, no, I didn't even know. You have to understand, I didn't know enough about this business to know a hit from a not hit. For ten years I was thinking like my mother did. My mother didn't think I had a real job until we got inducted into the Smithsonian and we showed up in the Encyclopedia Americana. Now you're talking—you saw something concrete. That was a big deal, especially to my parents who bought my encyclopedias one book at a time so I could have a set. So to be in Encyclopedia Americana—now that was the first time I really said, "we got something here." That's when I knew we had something lasting and that I wasn't going to have to go back to being a sub ever again.

In the early days of the show, watching Jim Henson work was absolutely amazing. Some of the things that we had to do were pretty strange. We had Marconi cameras and there were three of them. If you would punch them up on the video switcher, they weren't true to color. Over on one screen my dress was pink, over here my dress was orange and over here my dress was red, all in the same scene. Caroll Spinney (Big Bird) called them macaroni cameras—they were not good. Our crew was very inexperienced and, honestly, we all were. From a technical standpoint, the first thing that we were glad that happened due to the success of the show was when we got better cameras in the studio. They made the whole show much easier to shoot.

The next thing that only happened because of our cast was that they couldn't light us properly. If they put too much light on the bird, he flared on camera. Then they would adjust for that but then they would take a shot of me and all you'd see were my teeth and my eyes. Shooting an interracial group plus the bird was such a technical problem. They had to re-dye the bird's feathers darker so there wasn't such a range of color. That was really because they had to put enough light on us so they can see our features, not just our eyes and teeth.

Compared to the rest of us, Jim Henson had a lot of television experience. Jim had been on the *Tonight Show*. He had done commercials and he had regular spots on prime time programs. His work was pretty amazing because understood how to organize things to get what he wanted for his characters. The thing that most people wouldn't know is that Jim and most of the puppeteers were tall. They wanted the puppets' stages tall so that they weren't always working on their knees. The puppets' stages were big, the puppets were big, and the puppeteers even wore some of them. Cookie Monster—they put him on! Cookie Monster's hand is the puppeteer's real hand. The puppets were big and that was one of the accommodations that had to be made to the set. I remember the puppets' stages being very tall so that Jim and the other puppeteers could stand up and work the Muppets.

In the beginning of the show, Jim Henson had a lot to do with how the show was formed. It didn't change into that; it started out that way. Once he became a part of *Sesame Street*, he put his passion and genius into the show. Many people don't realize that in the classic *Sesame Street* counting film series, "One Wedding Cake," when there was always a person falling down the stairs in the end—that was always Jim. He couldn't find a stuntman who would do that, so he had to do it himself. Many of the short films were Jim's that he actually filmed, wrote and edited. Many of those short thirty-second spots featured his kids who are now all grown up. He had a big, big influence on how the show looked. The show really evolved just as technology evolved. The concept of the show didn't really change, but what we could do and how we could teach it, that changed and I think it is still changing.

In the very early seasons of the show, most of the humans didn't really do that much with the Muppets when Jim was in the studio. Jim and the puppet pieces all taped on Fridays. Now Big Bird was there with us all the time, Oscar was there with us all the time and so was Cookie Monster. They were street puppets more or less that were usually used in the street scenes and we interacted with them often. However, for Jim's roll-ins, they took the studio for the whole day.

I was very lucky to be a part of a number of those roles as a voice actor. Some of the Muppets that I provided the voices for were Anything Muppets. Here's how Anything Muppets are described by the Muppet Wiki:

Anything Muppets (or "AMs", as they're referred to in the studio) are "empty" Muppet heads. Facial features, bodies and clothes can be added to make any kind of character. The corresponding family of monster puppets are known as the AM Monsters. A similar group of puppets known as Whatnots appeared on **The Muppet Show.** *Some Anything Muppets have also appeared in Muppet movies and specials.*

The Anything Muppets were introduced in the first episode of **Sesame Street,** *in a sketch involving Gordon. An Anything Muppet appeared without any facial features, and Gordon introduced her as an Anything Person and proceeded to give her and four other Anything Muppets who appeared in sequence eyes, noses, and hair to form a family.*

During the first seasons of **Sesame Street,** *they were known as "The Anything People," which could be anything they wanted. Usually the live actors, like Bob, would turn them into different characters. This concept was abandoned after a few seasons, although every once in a while an Anything Muppet character would take off his nose or lose his mustache.*

Although these puppets were usually used to create human characters, animals were also sometimes concocted from Anything Muppets, until the late 1980s, including the Tortoise and the Hare, the Three Little Pigs and Captain Vegetable. This practice could be seen in The Miss Muffet Play. Aliens, such as The Gonk and The Geefle, and monsters such as Bennett Snerf, Arlene Frantic, Fenwick, Rosemary and Pamela could also be made from Anything Muppets.

Main **Sesame Street** *characters that are made from Anything Muppets include Count von Count, Prairie Dawn, Mr. Johnson, Roosevelt Franklin, Guy Smiley, Lefty the Salesman, the Twiddlebugs, and Sherlock Hemlock.*

I lent my voice to various Muppet segments on *Sesame Street*, particularly in the early seasons. On the 8th episode of the first season (1969), I sang the voice of the mother Muppet in the song "Five People in My Family." I also provided the voice for the mother of Roosevelt Franklin, and the voice of a backup singer in the nonsense song "Mahna Mahna."

For the audience, there was a deeper sense of diversity that evolved from our show. It was interesting because when we started the show diversity wasn't a hot buzzword, but it was always there. The puppets that Jim used were not all the same. He named them "Muppets" because they weren't marionettes and they weren't puppets. They were different than what puppets on television looked like up until that point. They were different colors. They were different sizes. They were different styles. There is such a wide range of puppet types on the show. We have Big Bird who is a walk-around puppet. We have Mr. Snuffleupagus who had two people inside of the puppet. Then there is Elmo who actually is on a hand with rod arms. For Oscar, Caroll Spinney sort of wore him on his arm. Some of those puppets were so big that the actors actually put them on sort of like a costume. All of that spawned from Jim Henson's imagination. The diversity of *Sesame Street* was built right into all of the beloved Muppets.

If you look at the original cast members—we're white, we're black, and later on the show added Luis and Maria (Emilio Delgado and Sonia Manzano) who are Latino. Will Lee (Mr. Hooper) was a senior citizen, so there was age diversity too. When Will died, Northern Calloway, a young black actor who played David, took over Mr. Hooper's store. When *Sesame Street* contributor Emily Kingsley's son was born with Down syndrome, she campaigned for special needs children to be integrated into the population of characters on the show. They were kids who lived on that street and played together just like every other kid who was on the show. That also led to us having Tara on the show, who was in a titanium wheelchair and could pop wheelies and race down the street. They were just integrated into the community. *Sesame Street* has always been a diverse place and I hope it always will be.

Recently, my friend Emilio Delgado, who plays Luis on *Sesame Street,* reflected about how diversity on the show affected him:

As a Chicano actor, as a Latino actor in Hollywood in the late 1950s, it was very hard to break into the business. I graduated from high school in 1959 and immediately went to Hollywood trying to work, trying to get in to do this and do that. At that time it was really difficult to get any kind of a sizeable part that was representing a meaningful human being on television for a Latino or a Latina.

It was very hard and, sure, there had been others like Anthony Quinn. He was my idol at the time because he was the first Mexican American who made it big in Hollywood. Cesar Romero and Ricardo Montalbán and all those guys that had come before us. They had been the first wave of Latinos in Hollywood, but they only were allowed to play very stereotypical parts. All of these people, as famous and as successful as they were, were always being given the stereotypical roles of the Latin lover and the Apache. I had to admire them because they were Latinos,

Chicanos and they were working in Hollywood.

When I came along, my generation of actors wanted to get into the business and do something that would turn us into working actors. At the time the opportunities were very scarce, very scarce. For me, to get a job on a regular television show, that was the biggest thing that could happen to any Latino. I acted on a show in 1968 where I was a part of a Mexican-American family that took place in East L.A. and it was aired on PBS. That was the beginnings of showing Chicanos and Latinos as real people. I played the older son of the family and that was a good part.

That started me thinking that this type of non-stereotypical representation is important. We have to keep doing this. We have to keep showing ourselves and we have to keep representing ourselves as real people. When I got the job on **Sesame Street***, that's what I wanted to do. I just wanted to portray Luis as a regular human being. The opportunity was an immense opportunity because the people at Children's Television Workshop were willing to go along with anything that we were coming up with. We were just being regular people. Yeah, we had the scripts and they put the words in our mouths, but we interpreted those words in ways that were not stereotypical and that were much more natural than what we had seen on television* *in the past.*

Fortunately for me, Spanish had been my first language, so I had no problem with speaking Spanish and teaching Spanish on the show. Since the part of Luis depicted him as a Chicano from out West, I had to put the Spanish in there. That's when I started calling Big Bird "Pájaro." I'd always say, "Hey, Pájaro," which means bird. I think the work I did on the show and continue to do has changed the lives of so many people. I'm very proud of what we accomplished and what we did to bring diversity into so many homes in America.

Emilio Delgado, Luis on **Sesame Street,** *1971-Present*

Part 4: Life As A TV Star

*On set and on the road with Matt Robinson who played Gordon during
the first three seasons of* Sesame Street.

On set in the 1970s with Bob McGrath, Matt Robinson and Will Lee.

On set in the late 1970s.

Studying a script on set in the 1970s.

Backstage with Bob McGrath and some of the kids reviewing a street scene from Sesame Street *in the 1970s.*

In 1974, Fischer Price made a line of toys based on Sesame Street. *Here's a picture of me as one of the "Little People." These are the only toys ever made of the humans from the show. These are also the only Little People modeled after real people.*

After a while I started to get recognized when I went out. It was really something. The show was catching on and growing in popularity. It was never grownups that recognized me though. It was always children. Sometimes they just recognized my voice. I could go pretty much where I wanted to. But if I went to the wrong places, like a toy store or something like that, I knew I'd be in trouble. There were always certain times of the day not to go into the grocery store because I knew there would be little kids there riding in the carts. Children who are fans of the show always recognize you there and it's very hard not to stop and talk to all of them. People still always recognize me today, but now it's usually not the children. Now it's the adults who were children when they watched the show recognizing me. It's amazing when you realize that multiple generations of people have watched our show and that some of our first viewers are now grandparents.

One of the ways that I met many fans and viewers of the show was by doing public appearances. The JC Penney department stores had the exclusive rights to *Sesame Street* clothing back in the early days of the show. This started in 1975 and the whole cast would make appearances in stores all over the United States. The JC Penney tour went on and on. It was generally held during the back to school season. They would like to have us in the store for back to school because the marketing people understood that we drew a whole family. The children were not going to drive there by themselves; the parents would have to take them. It wasn't lost on the marketing people that a whole family would come to see me and the rest of the cast and probably buy other things when they were in the store. The appearances were a lot of fun because they would bring out a lot of people and I would meet so many families from all over the country. Hearing their stories about watching the show and how it was affecting their children was inspiring and amazing. I always enjoyed talking to everyone I met.

One of my most memorable times I had on the tour happened very early in the morning on a day when we performed and did a meet and greet at a mall in Dallas, Texas. On occasions like that, I would always try out my equipment to make sure that the tape deck was going to play and that the microphones would work when it was time to sing. I remember that "Who Are the People in Your Neighborhood" was playing as I tested the tape player. Then in the food court way in the back, I could see a mother and a son. When the music started playing, he jumped up and started running. The mother couldn't catch him. He came running up to me. I had a firefighter's hat, some boots and a mailbag for the people in the neighborhood part of the show. He quickly put the firefighter's hat on and the mother had this funny look on her face. He was a little older, but I didn't think anything of it, so I said,

"Boy, you're here so early. You can really get a good seat."

I turned off the tape because I was only checking it to make sure it worked and then I quickly headed backstage. When I came back for the show at 11:00 am, they were sitting in the front row, and I said,

"Oh, you got yourself a good seat!"

"Who Are the People in Your Neighborhood" was about the third song in the show. When it started playing, the boy walked up and put the hat on again and started singing. Then he reached for my microphone. That's when I said, "Wait a minute. Wait a minute. You've got to go get your own show if you want the mic. You can't have my mic."

So he quickly left the stage. I saw the mother leaving out of the corner of my eye and I remember wondering where she was going. The boy sat down and we went on with the show. After the show ended, the manager of the mall came out and said,

"I'm going to sit with him. His mother wants to see you in the ladies' room." I remember saying, "Oh my God. I wonder if she thought I was making fun of her kid. I would never do that." Then I said, "Oh great. I'm going to get beat up in the ladies' room in Dallas, Texas." I slowly walked into the bathroom not knowing what to expect. When I finally saw her I realized that she was crying. She went on to tell me that her son is autistic and that I'm his favorite on the show. She also said that he talks to me when I'm on camera. When he saw my picture in the paper he said, "I want to go see Susan."

She said, "We came early because he doesn't like crowds. So, we were going to sit way back there in the food court. But when he saw you and he came running to you and began talking to you, I was shocked. Then when he got up and started singing in front of the other children I was stunned. I never he thought he would be that high functioning and I didn't want him to see me crying."

And so then I cried. We were both in there crying together. To me it was so important that we had touched that child in that way. Often, autism will let people relate to television more than the actual person. But he came and talked to me and that's what made his mother cry. It was an absolutely amazing experience and it is a memory that always helps to remind me that we will never actually be able to fully understand what a person experiences when they watch our show.

Because JC Penney had the license for the *Sesame Street* products, I went everywhere there was a JC Penney store in the continental United States and Hawaii. I traveled all over the country for a few years until they no longer had the license. I think that the tour helped me understand that this show really had an impact on people. When you're in a studio doing it, you have no idea what people are experiencing on the other side of the screen. You send it out through the television, but you don't really know that people really know who you are until they come up and smile at you. Then once you realize they'd stand in a line to talk to you, it's pretty remarkable.

It's amazing the poor planning that happened sometimes during that tour. It's a children's show. Why are you putting the meet and greet in the china department? We had the china buyers so crazy that when all these people showed up, they made us go to the parking lot in the heat. I remember one time when there were 1,500 people at the event. They didn't have enough security and they sure shouldn't have put it in the china department. I remember that we were out in the parking lot of a mall and a lady said to me,

"If you love children, please take what my son has for you," and I said, "Okay." He opened his hand and his M&Ms had bonded together in a big mountain. He said,

"Hi. I brought this for you, Susan."

I said, "Oh, thank you." His mother was nodding along, "Thank you." Things like that seemed to happen all of the time.

Another time a little boy came up to me and opened his hand and said,

"Open your hand. I brought you something."

I said, "Oh boy."

I opened my hand and he put two quarters in my hand. I said,

"Where did you get this?"

He said, "Oh, it was just laying around."

He was wet up to his armpit. He'd taken the money out of the wishing well in the middle of the mall. Then he said, "It was just laying there, doing nothing, so I brought it to you." And I said,

"Oh, great."

As I was doing a lot of JC Penney's appearances, I got recognized much more. In terms of my own privacy, I had one thing in my favor. Little kids think you live in their TV, so they never expect to see you in places like the grocery store or at the cleaners. In my neighborhood in Teaneck, New Jersey, where I lived then, everyone was very nice and really left me alone. Most of the time, they didn't really recognize me. Once in a while, it was pretty embarrassing.

I'll never forget this story. Everyone knows that women take little boys to the ladies' room and ladies' room stalls never go all the way to the floor. One day, all of a sudden, I was in a stall and there was a little face peeking under the door wanting to interview me and ask me all sorts of questions.

I said, "Uh, I'm kind of busy right now. Where is your mother?"

The little boy said, "Oh, she's over there holding my coat."

Then I said, "Ah, well, can you wait until I come out?"

He said, "Yeah, okay."

Another time, I had a nearly fatal experience with a loving kindergarten class that almost loved me to the ground while their teachers stood there and held their coats. They love you, but if they love you enough and there are enough of them, that could be fatal.

Today, when I get recognized it's very different. When I meet fans of the show that grew up watching me, I really enjoy talking to them. I love hearing about everything they are doing with their lives. I also enjoy when they tell me how the show led them on a career path, like becoming a teacher. It's very heartwarming and rewarding for me when I realize that portraying Susan had an impact on so many people's lives.

Getting recognized for being on the show led me to a project that I am still very proud of. One day back in 1970, I was in a delicatessen after church, and these two little girls walked up and said, "Hi, Susan," and sat down and began to eat my food.

Their father said, "What are you doing?"

They said, "We're talking to our friend Susan."

They were already eating my potatoes. I remember he said,

"Excuse me. I'm sorry. How do you know my daughters?"

I said, "You ask them."

He said, "How do you know her?"

The girls said, "Oh, she's on *Sesame Street*. She's our friend Susan."

Then he said, "Really?"

I said, "Mm-hmm."

So he invited himself to sit down. When he finished buying my breakfast, because his daughters had eaten it all up, he could see the way these children related to me. He figured that a lot of children would and he was right. He was a businessman named Murray Ross and he ended up executive producing my record album project, "Susan Sings Songs from *Sesame Street* with the Children's Chorus."

The thing that made this project just wonderful was Joe Raposo's music. Joe was a composer, songwriter, pianist, television writer and lyricist. He really is best known for his work on our show and I met him while I was working on the first season of *Sesame Street*. Many of you may know this already, but Joe wrote the theme song for *Sesame Street*, as well as classic songs such as "Bein' Green" and "C is for Cookie." He also wrote all of the words and music on my album along with Jeffery Moss and Clark Gessner.

Joe prided himself in not writing kiddie music. He wrote good music and he got some members of *The Tonight Show* band to play it for my album. I mean that was like such a dream come true. When Johnny Carson moved *The Tonight Show* from New York to LA, not all of the members of *The Tonight Show* band went with him. A lot of them stayed and became studio musicians in New York City. They played on a lot of *Sesame Street's* early music recordings.

Being around that level of creativity when you're in the throes of doing an album and you're as new to the business as I was, was amazing. From time to time, I found myself just dumbfounded. I knew that these were people who had big time credits. Joe Raposo had the longest running off Broadway show at that time. The fact that he could get members from *The Tonight Show* Band to play our tracks showed how respected he was. We had the best studio musicians in the world playing the *Sesame Street* music.

That level of musicians playing our music on my album was simply amazing. Joe really did it all. He arranged it. He even did the contracting of the players on the album. All I did was just walk in there and sing my song like a big time star. It was very amazing to me because I hadn't had that kind of opportunity before. The fact that the project came into being was amazing as well. It was those two little girls that I mentioned before who made this all happen. I think they were four and five years old at the time. They insisted on eating my breakfast at a delicatessen on Broadway and their father kept saying, "how do they know you?" I think he thought I was somebody's babysitter or day care teacher or something. He didn't know why the girls knew me well enough to eat up all my food. He was the one who put the record deal together and he got Scepter Records to distribute the album. I introduced him to Joe and my attorney. Then, I was done with it. After that, all I did was show up and sing my songs. It was truly a dream come true and once again, I was **Occupying My Dream.**

I traveled the whole country promoting the record. That was a first for me with a record. Scepter Records distributed the album and set up the tour. That was Florence Greenberg's record label. Her label recorded acts like Dionne Warwick and The Shirelles and helped turn them into to nationally known stars. They knew how to distribute my album and I trusted them to put me in all the right places. During the tour, if they wanted me in a city like Chicago, I'd fly there and they'd pick me up in a limo. It was so exciting for me. They brought me to the stores where I was supposed to be. Wherever the record company sent me, I met children and families who wanted to buy the record. This was 1970 and *Sesame Street* had only been on for one season. Because of the tour, I met so many people who were watching the show and I truly felt like a star.

Because of the album, I even got to appear as a featured guest on *The Flip Wilson Show*. I knew Flip through my husband Pete Long. Pete had promoted his comedy club shows and Flip performed at the Apollo Theater where my husband was the manager. Flip had tons of favors to pay back to people who helped him get to where he was at the time and I really think this was one of them.

For me this was a chance to promote *Sesame Street* and my album. The show aired on October 15, 1970 on NBC. We were just in the midst of season 2 of *Sesame Street* and it was a very overwhelming and exciting time in my career. This was national television and people all over the country could see this show, even all of my friends and family back in Paw Paw, Michigan. I appeared on the show with Big Bird and Oscar the Grouch and I got to perform a number of songs from my album. I was accompanied on the show by Sunday's Child, which was a music group of young, very talented female African American singers. Raymond Burr was also a guest on that show and it was absolutely amazing to meet him and to work with someone who had had so much success in show business. One of the things that stands out to me most about being on *The Flip Wilson Show* is that we had to lip-sync everything. All of the songs had been pre-recorded. I learned pretty quickly that I wasn't going to be able to sing the songs the same way I did on my album because they would be very hard to lip-sync to. I kept it simple and I think the performances turned out great.

Overall, the experience is so hard to articulate in words. It was so incredible. It wasn't long before this that I had been trying to get any acting, singing or dancing job that I could. It wasn't long before this that I was living in Paw Paw. If you'd like to see the episode, it's available on DVD now and it's titled *The Flip Wilson Show Episode 5, Season 1*. For me, viewing it now is like traveling back in time to the beginning of my career on *Sesame Street*. I am so fortunate that so much of my career has been preserved on videotape and that it is available for a whole new generation of viewers.

It was a wonderful time for me and I thought that it would lead to many more solo projects. It unfortunately didn't. Mainly because the Children's Television Workshop started to have the cast record its own record albums. So I wasn't really allowed to make albums like this one anymore. The show was starting to become so popular that the producers started to think of ways to capitalize on the success of the show. Record albums featuring the cast and the *Sesame Street* Muppets were just one of the ways they did just that. I wasn't angry that I couldn't record another solo project; I embraced the cast albums that we recorded. They were truly great.

The cover art for "Susan Sings Songs from Sesame Street."

This album reached #86 on Billboard's Top LPs chart in 1970. It was nominated for a Grammy Award for Best Recording for Children, but lost to "The Sesame Street Book & Record" which I also appeared on.

Meeting families at a department store while on tour promoting my album back in 1970. I met thousands of children during this tour.

On my record tour in 1970, visiting an elementary school.

The same year my album debuted so did "The *Sesame Street* Book & Record*"* which was the first of many *Sesame Street* albums I would perform on over the years. Even though my album was successful and even nominated for a Grammy, it was really my first and last solo project. "The *Sesame Street* Book & Record" was certified Gold and beat my album for the Grammy for Best Recording for Children in 1970. The album reached #86 on Billboard's Top LPs chart. My recording career had an amazing start and I have enjoyed working on all of the *Sesame Street* albums I had the opportunity to be a part of over the years.

Some of the songs from *Sesame Street* have become iconic and part of Americana. They are really the completion of my dream as an eight year old out harvesting crops who saw herself as a musical performer. I always saw myself basically as a singer. Much of my work prior to *Sesame Street* was singing. I had limited myself in my head to being a record act. So, my focus was always trying to get a record contract, but you see that wasn't really where I actually got exposure. I got it on television, but I never saw myself being on television. On the television programs that I saw as a young girl, everyone was white unless they were playing something like a maid. So I didn't see myself on TV. Out in the country we got such bad reception, it was all fuzzy and television just wasn't something that I watched much or focused on. I just really only wanted to be a record act.

The first time I really realized on a personal level that I was famous was when I called my mother and said,

"We're riding in the Macy's Thanksgiving Day Parade. We have a float, and we'll be on camera by 9:00."

I knew exactly where my mother was. She was in the kitchen making pumpkin pies because that's where I would have been as a kid, sitting in the kitchen with my mother, watching the Macy's Thanksgiving Day Parade. That was the moment I realized I was famous. I was on the float, not watching the floats in the parade on television. That was an amazing feeling that I will never forget.

On the **Sesame Street** *float in the Macy's Thanksgiving Day Parade.*

I came to a realization that I had underestimated the importance of *Sesame Street* in popular culture of the 1970's. You can get so involved in doing a project that you don't even know the impact of it. I didn't realize the impact of *Sesame Street* in context of my always wanting to be a record act until I met Martha Reeves of Martha and the Vandellas, who sang "Dancing in the Street." I told her about my audition for Motown. She said,

"Girl, you ought to be glad you went on to New York."

I said, "Why?" She said, "You're a big star and you're on television everyday and I'm an oldie but a goodie."

I said, "Wow, that puts it in perspective, doesn't it?"

She said, "Yeah, girl. I would trade my career any day to be on television everyday."

See, sometimes you're so used to something you don't even understand the real impact of it until people say something like that to you. That was quite amazing and also very insightful.

PBS wasn't what it is today when we started *Sesame Street*. You weren't even able to get it very well in Michigan. If you didn't have a big tower or something, it came in fuzzy. So my poor Dad, my mother had him up on the roof. Daddy was a welder, so he had some other apparatus he put together that he placed on the roof so that they could get the show. But the fact that the reception was so bad and that every season I had to wait for a new contract made my parents so nervous. They were glad I was a teacher because they knew I could always go get myself a sub license and teach.

I don't think my parents realized the importance of my work on the show until *Sesame Street* was put into the *Encyclopedia Americana* and they opened up to that page and there was a picture of me. My parents bought my set of encyclopedias one book at a time just so I could have a whole set. Back then having an encyclopedia was so important. That was when my mother said,

"Well, I guess you made it. You're in the encyclopedia."

Then the Smithsonian inducted the show into the American History Museum. The funny thing about the Smithsonian Institute doing this for the 10th anniversary of the show was that they had Charlie Rosen design the house and they built it to his specs. Then they came and measured us and made wax mannequins of each cast member. They also took the clothes that we wore on television and put them on the mannequins. Well, then they invited us to the opening of the exhibit, which was a very wonderful experience.

I remember that we freaked out a kindergarten class that was at the opening because we were there and the mannequins were there and they didn't know who to look at. They were screaming. It wasn't exactly the reaction we expected. Like I said before, little kids think you live in their TV so when they see you in real life sometimes things get out of control. But the best story comes from my niece, who got up in her fourth grade class and said, "My Aunt Loretta is in an institution." I said to her mother, "Could you tell your daughter I am an institution, not I'm in an institution?" She said, "Yes, the Smithsonian Institution."

The *Kalamazoo Gazette* was a daily newspaper that people all over Michigan read every day. Kalamazoo is about twenty miles from Paw Paw. Our paper in Paw Paw only came out once a week. As we were getting inducted into the Smithsonian, the *Kalamazoo Gazette* sent a reporter and a photographer to my mother and father's house to interview me. I was sitting at the kitchen table and my mother had her back to us. She was cooking something. The reporter asked me a question and as I opened my mouth, my mother answered. So the reporter asked me another question and I opened my mouth, and my mother answered. So the reporter was very confused and I remember saying,

"It's her house." I felt like one of Jim Henson's puppets. I'd open my mouth and somebody else's voice would come out.

Celebrating ten years of Sesame Street *in 1979 outside our offices at* **Lincoln Center, New York City.**

The next day, she got the paper and she said,

"This is the best interview you ever gave."

I wanted to say,

"It is the best interview I never gave."

She knew all the answers to the questions so she just answered.

Looking back, I think my parents were proud of me, but they were proud of all of their kids. My father was good at saying that people would try to make me different than the rest and they wouldn't allow that. My father would always say, "I'm proud of all my kids. None of them went to jail," and he'd stand up and leave. That would be the end of the interview if they start to take that track.

I was on *Sesame Street* probably just a couple of years and, over time, you realize that your friends get you into stuff. A friend of a mine said to the head of the Urban Ed Center, an experimental center at the University of Massachusetts Amherst Campus,

"I know this lady on *Sesame Street*."

The head of the center said,

"We're going to have a symposium on education. Ask her if she'll come and speak."

So this friend comes back and tells me,

"They are doing this week-long symposium. People can earn a grad credit if they go to all the things that are being offered and write a reflection paper. Would you speak? They want to know about *Sesame Street*."

I said, "Okay."

They didn't anticipate the number of people that wanted to hear me speak, so the overflow of people was tremendous. They should have put me in a bigger room. They didn't. So then the overflow rooms had to be classrooms and I was on camera and the students had to view my talk on monitors in each room. That was kind of interesting. To see that kind of interest on a college campus for a kids' show was pretty amazing.

I found out later that all of the early childhood education students were required to go to my talk. So during my talk, I said that I didn't think that schools of education did a very good job preparing teachers to teach in urban schools and I relayed some of my experiences. I also relayed the fact that when I went back to my undergrad school, not one person who was teaching teachers to teach ever taught off that campus.

All of a sudden, I hear, "Ooh." You know how little kids do when you're about to get in trouble? "Ooooh." And somebody was approaching me from behind. I could see him in my peripheral vision. I said, "Do they have a uniform on? Are they coming to get me?" I said, "Don't worry. I got my plane ticket home. I've been put out of better places than this." This man comes up and says,

"Hi, I'm Dwight Allen. I'm Dean of the School of Urban Ed."

I said, "Okay." He said, "So, if you think you can do a better job of teaching, why don't you come up here and teach a class?"

Me and my big mouth. I thought to myself, Okay. Okay? I'm working. I'm an actor working on a television show. We go into the studio in the morning and we come out at night. When am I going to teach? But I said I would do it anyway. So I taught a class called

Media and the Classroom Teacher. That particular campus had an agreement with Hampshire, Sarah Lawrence, Amherst College and other UMass campuses. People from any of those schools could take a class. My class was so full that they had to do the overflow room again. They gave me a block of independent grad credits and that's what started grad school for me, but I had no intention of going back to school.

Back then on *Sesame Street*, Friday was Muppet day. If you weren't in something with the Muppets, you automatically had a Friday off, so I told them I would teach on Friday. I was living in Teaneck, New Jersey at the time, so I had to take the bus from uptown Port Authority, get off in Hartford, and get onto a Peter Pan bus. Any bus that's got a guy in leotards on the side instead of a greyhound is already suspect. Some days it took us longer than others, but I would take the bus up there and teach my class and come back. Then as I started going to school, I could only go on Fridays because of our shooting schedule. This went on until I graduated in 1973.

My degree is my future. It's my *Sesame Street* and beyond. It's my future because there are a couple of things that are significant about it. It makes me want to have my own learning centers and I have the credibility because I have the credentials. It will allow me to train people and let them get credentials because I can sign off on their experimental work.

Visiting a 5th grade classroom in Manalapan, NJ to talk about my career, June 2013

I ultimately want a company called Innovations in Education. What I will do with my learning centers is give people a place to try new things. What always used to shut me down from the time I was a sub would be people saying, "We don't do it like that. There's too much laughter coming out of your classroom. We don't have enough money for that." I want to be the person that could give a micro-grant to somebody who thinks they have an innovative way to teach students that I'm learning to call "educationally resistant students."

See, everyone wants to label kids, and I'm anti-labeling people. Who sets what's norm? What is the normal? Why label kids outside of normal? Who says that's normal? Who says that? So I've come up with an expression, "educationally resistant student." A lot of times they're bright enough to resist the garbage that's being put on them. I'd be mad too if the educational system didn't serve me better than it serves some of these kids. Our brightest and our best are in the joint. They're in jail because we drug them or put them out.

I want to be in a position to let people who think they can do a better job working with these educationally resistant students have a place to try it out. And I especially like the use of technology because my first successful class that I did outside of *Sesame Street* was in an alternative high school. It's called Nelson Mandela Community School. It's in Mt. Vernon, New York. The community called it "Last Chance High" because there was a judge that actually sentenced kids to that school. He'd say, "This is going to be your last chance or you got to go to the joint and serve your time. I'm not talking about residential detention. I'm talking about you really got to go to prison." So there were more parole officers at the school than faculty because every kid had a parole officer.

I taught "Team Up for Success Using Television Production" because these kids knew how to double-team people, but they didn't know how to work like a crew. There was something about producing a television show that taught them to do what they had never done before. One mother said, "Dr. Long, those boys—when they came to my front door, it scared me 'til I realized they were there to get my son because he had all the props and he wasn't going to go to school that day. They said, 'Yes, you are. Come on.'" She said, "They got him up. I couldn't get him up." They learned about being a crew. It was an incredibly rewarding experience for all of us.

The thing about it was they loved being on camera so much that they were motivated to do all the jobs they had. They had to earn the right to be on camera, so they had to be the crew for each other's projects.

When I reflect about my career on *Sesame Street* it brings to mind the old vaudeville joke where a tourist comes up to a news vendor and says, "Can you tell me how to get to Carnegie Hall?" He just looks up and he says, "Yes. Practice." Our question is "Can you tell me how to get to *Sesame Street*?" My answer is "Dream." That's what *Sesame Street* has been for me. It's been the culmination of my dream. But what it has done for me is given me a platform to dream beyond *Sesame Street*.

I think Susan has been a role model for women. It's interesting because you've got to remember our target audiences are interested in black and white. I've been on live shoots where they walked up to the blonde from the marketing department and said "are you Susan?" So little kids don't see color, they barely see gender. They knew Gordon didn't have any hair and Susan had the hair. They are so pure that what you're sending them heart to heart is more important than gender or color to them. They like Susan, thank goodness. There was something about me to like and there was something about the way they wrote my character that little kids out in the street thought I should sit down with them on the stoop and start talking to them. This got to be kind of sticky in an airport when your flight is boarding and they want you to sit there and talk to them because they're used to seeing you do that on the show.

I think that a lot of my own personality and who I am is portrayed in the character of Susan. They hired who they wanted those characters to be. Bob from the Midwest and me, I'm from the Midwest too. They made us write the backstory for each of our own characters. For instance they wanted us to make up where this character was before the first day on *Sesame Street*, and we gave that to the writers. I decided that since I was from the Midwest, so was Susan. They made me a nurse, so I was a nurse. I had an intact family, I grew up on a farm—Susan was very much Loretta. The backstory was very much mine.

When I look back at old episodes of the show it makes me cry. I can really look back at almost two thirds of my life just by watching different seasons of the show. I think that we all did a good job of representing someone that we could be proud of. I think for the cast across the board, the writers wrote us well. At its core the show showed that poor city people cared about each other and really liked each other. I think that came over well.

The cast of the show is like a second family to me. Just within the last few years we haven't been together a lot but we generally spend a lot of time together. We used to laugh about having big calendars around because when you come in to work, it's dark and when you leave, it's dark, so you lose all track of time. There were years in there where we went, huh? We're on season 30? It went faster than you could imagine. As we are getting to be seniors now, some of us are disappearing, and that's getting to be sad. I don't want to go to one more memorial. It's kind of hard to say goodbye to so many old friends whom I've spent so much of my life with.

Visiting the Jim Henson's statue at the University of Maryland

in May 2014.

Part 5: "Goodbye Mr. Hooper"

Shooting the Sesame Street *pilot shows in July 1969 with*

Will Lee, Bob McGrath and Garret Saunders.

Five pilot episodes were shot to use for audience testing purposes.
These episodes were never aired on television.

In 1982, Will Lee died very early in the beginning of the taping season. I said we can't really do anything right away. It was too soon. We spent the year developing the messages. I interviewed various experts in the area of death. We did research to find out what children knew about death and then we worked with them to create actual messages.

The critical things that the experts wanted us to say had to do with, "Say he's dead, not he's passed away, resting, any of those kinds of things, but be very specific that he's dead, that he's not coming back," because kids have a tendency to think that death passes. If you have seen the segment, we worked through those issues of Big Bird expecting Mr. Hooper to come back even though the word "dead" had been said.

The fact that the person will be missed, the fact that the person will not be replaced but your needs will be met was a critical kind of a message that needed to be given to the children. We can't replace a person—they were really special—but you're going to have your milkshakes and things like that. Those were the critical messages that we did. It was an incredible emotional experience in the studio.

When I think about what Susan was, basically she was the mother. She played the mother role throughout in terms of the whole show. In the very beginning when they were developing the Susan character, they didn't give her any children; they gave her a husband, but they didn't give her any children. The thinking was that they wanted her to be the mother image for all the children and the Muppets as well. In that particular piece, the only person that actually got up and really stroked and touched Big Bird was Susan, being that mother, being that mother image. It was very important and critical that she connect with the Muppet in that way, connect with the child in that way, and comfort that child in that way.

We were concerned about whether or not this particular episode was going to have a negative impact on children, and so we actually did research to find that out. We had children watch it and leave with their parents, and then followed up to find out what had actually happened to the children. Did they have repeated dreams of death or were they talking about death? Were they afraid or frightened?

We also tried to find out, "What did you say?" The piece just said, "Because..." It just said, "Because," so the parents could fill in what happened to Mr. Hooper. They filled in their religious interpretations of what happened. All those kinds of elements of religion and beliefs about life and death, the parents could fill those things in, and so the piece was written in a way where it could be understood. We saw ourselves, from our research, that the parents filled in the gaps, depending on the age of the children and things like that. We felt comfortable saying that, from a research point of view, we feel like this is a piece that can work. That was how that went, and then we received an Emmy for that segment. Norman Stiles wrote it and he did an excellent job of really capturing it, and the cast did a beautiful job of acting.

Dr. Valaria Lovelace, Director of Research,

Sesame Street, *1982-1996*

All of the human stars of the show were in that scene. Everybody knew the lines.

Jon Stone said, "Don't you take any scripts in there. You have to memorize it perfectly."

He was hard on me. There was nothing wrong with that. Honestly, it was a novel thing for me to actually know the script. I said it mostly my own way, but this script was so well-written that he wanted it just the way it was because it was probably one of the greatest scripts we ever did.

Will Lee was special to all of us on the show. He was a master teacher. He even taught James Earl Jones.

The last time I worked with James Earl Jones, probably about ten years ago, he said that if it wasn't for Will Lee (who played Mr. Hooper) he wouldn't be an actor. He said, "he was my teacher, he gave me the confidence to actually go out on a stage and perform because I was a stutterer."

Will Lee really taught us all. He was great. I loved working with him. When we first went on the air he wasn't used to people ad-libbing like the puppeteers did. He was used to scripts. For instance, I'd say something off script. I would just think of a line that was a funnier line because I knew the characters and what they would say. I would say it that way and when it was time for his next line, he would have to stop and say, "where are you going? What are you saying?"

He got used to that after a couple months. We would surprise him when we would just make up the lines. We'd stick to the story but we said it in our own way so he just didn't recognize it.

That's one of the problems when you do memorize the script; you have to memorize who's going to speak next. That's one of the hardest parts—I think more than your knowing your lines. One thing that I loved about Will, he knew we needed help and we were such novices we didn't even know it. He would put us all in a room and he'd make us rehearse. He'd make us run lines and he would come get us because we didn't even have enough sense to go get him.

He was such a sweet man. I think he really came to love working on our show, because it became his show too. He was the grandfather figure on set. He really loved us all.

Caroll Spinney, Big Bird and Oscar the Grouch, 1969-Present

I always say that the two best shows we ever did were the "Goodbye Mr. Hooper" episode and "Christmas Eve on **Sesame Street.** *" We were fortunate that we were in a hiatus period when Will Lee passed away. It was fortunate for the research department and the writers because it gave them the time to do all the research that was necessary to help kids understand death and dying.*

The writers had tried something about death before. This was different—it's not just like having your gold fish die. This was somebody. At first the producers were going to say that Mr. Hooper retired and was going to go live with his sister in Florida. They had established part of this in the script some time before. Then they said, "that's not fair." These kids know and love him. They really needed to know what happened to him. They also needed to know how to handle something like this, especially if there was someone close to them who passed away. One of the most important goals of the script was to establish that when a person dies they never come back.

We barely were able to get through the scene. We rehearsed it with Jon Stone for a couple of hours, which is unusual; we never spend that much time on one scene. We did it totally dry with no emotion whatsoever. Finally, when Jon said, "we'll go to tape now," we did it straight through in one take. All of those tears that came out and all of the emotional things you see on screen, none of that was acting on anybody's part. It was all straight from the heart and from our gut.

I think that was one of the all time great shows. I think even the networks all realized that, which is evident in the fact that they even promoted the broadcast of the show. They had seen it and realized what an impact it would make on millions of kids. That was a part of television history that I think all of us were very happy to be a part of.

Bob McGrath, Bob on **Sesame Street,** *1969-Present*

The script was beautifully crafted by Norman Stiles, the head writer of the show at the time. Everyone involved had the same kind of feeling of loss and real reverence for Will Lee, who was a part of our family. This was not about acting. We didn't have to act or prepare except to learn the few lines. Actually, I went off on the lines. I just couldn't remember them. Every time I've seen the scene, I'm reminded that I didn't know my lines. In the scene when Loretta walks up, I was suppose to have said something that I just couldn't even remember. It was just so emotional. Loretta actually said the lines for me. Thank you, Loretta. I've never really thanked you for that.

It was such an incredible moment for all of us to say goodbye to one of our dearest friends and colleagues. We did it in front of America. It was so wonderful to have it aired on Thanksgiving that year so that it would be a moment that was shared among families at a special time. It provided a very special kind of teaching moment for families. It was highly recognized as being a real groundbreaking moment not just for our show but television itself.

Roscoe Orman, Gordon on **Sesame Street,** *1974-Present*

Death is hard for everyone and especially hard for children to understand. When we dealt with the death of Mr. Hooper on the show we were really breaking new ground. I think that the producers did a wonderful job and I think it's one of the aspects of our show that I'm the proudest of. At the show, we have a research division that actually consists of educational researchers and PhD's in education. For this episode, they worked on how to explain death to little children in a way that's honest but doesn't freak them out. The show also has an advisory board, which includes some of the heaviest hitters in child psychology and folks from the Harvard School of Education. They all came and sat in a room with the cast and the writers.

They really hammered out an approach that said we're not going to say he's going to live with the angels and God took him and all that. We're going to say he died. The producers were very careful about when the show aired. It aired over Thanksgiving weekend in 1983, so they knew there would be a lot of adults in the home and the child wouldn't see the show by themselves. They were careful to send out talking points for parents to go ahead and say to their child, "Remember this is what happened to grandma or grandpa?" Or, "Remember when your Poppy died?" They gave them specific ways to be there for the children. They didn't give us ways to be there for us though—it was very hard for the entire cast and crew.

We got through it. Big Bird, our resident child, asked the questions and said, "I understand it but I don't like it." We said, "We don't like it either Big Bird, but we'll always have him with us."

Carroll Spinney, who plays Big Bird, is a fine artist. He was going to school to study fine arts and paying his way doing puppets and it flipped around on him. Well, he had done caricatures of each of us

147

and he brought them to us as part of the scene. We were sitting in the arbor and then Big Bird started looking for Mr. Hooper. "Where's Mr. Hooper I want to give him this." Gordon said, "Well Big Bird, don't you remember, Mr. Hooper died." Then there was dead silence. "What do you mean, he's coming back, right?" said Big Bird. The research showed that you have to process something like this through for little kids, because people leave them and go in and out of their lives all the time. That was one of the key teaching points: no he's not coming back, he died.

After we shot the scene the director, Lisa Simon, came out crying and said,

"Well there's a few things wrong, do any of you want to do it over?"

We all said no and ran for our dressing rooms. We just got through it. It was an incredibly difficult time.

Will was more than a friend. He was to us what Jim Henson was to the puppeteers. Will was a very fine actor and an excellent teacher. Not only did he train James Earl Jones, he trained a lot of the guys when they came back from the Korean War and could get acting classes on the GI Bill. He was their teacher down in the Village. He was a wonderful actor, so he really took us all under his wing and we used to call him the man of a thousand takes. He was the one who really showed us, at least he showed me, how to be on camera, because even though I had taken acting classes before, working on television is different.

He had a Broadway background but he also had the big range. Thank goodness, he was kind and smart enough to put us all through many rehearsals. He would rehearse us before we'd go on the floor. He'd put us all in one dressing room and make us run lines. He'd come around to us and make us run lines because we didn't have enough sense to run lines. He knew that if the camera didn't fall off the tripod or a puppeteer didn't get caught in the shot, the shoot was moving on. He helped us be the best prepared we could be so that we could look the best that we could be. Looking back, he was a big help to us all. When you're in the middle of doing a scene, it would be like okay, here comes Will again, we've got to run lines. We wouldn't have known to come to him. To this day I am so thankful and grateful for what he taught me. Even now, thirty years later, I still miss him dearly.

Unfortunately, eight years later we lost Jim Henson. When Jim died it was devastating. For one thing, we didn't expect him to go so early, that was most of it. It was just so sudden. For me personally, I feel like he really didn't have a chance to complete all of his work and he had not completed his mission on Earth. However, God decided that it was his time to go and that was hard for everyone to accept.

After Jim died, it was harder for the puppeteers than the civilians because, first of all, they retired his voice. Nobody would do Ernie. The other puppeteers could do it, but nobody would do it. The Henson kids felt that their dad wouldn't want Ernie to just disappear. So, they had auditions and eventually Steve Whitmire took over Ernie in 1993.

For me, it really felt funny when we were at Carnegie Hall in 2012. I performed as part of Jim Henson's Musical World, which was a celebration of his work. We were accompanied on stage by the New York Pops and they had this big picture of him looking down on all of us on stage as we sang songs from *Sesame Street*. That was pretty awesome. There were puppeteers there that had never met each other because they were in different shows. The Canadian puppeteers from *Fraggle Rock* didn't know the English company. Then the *Sesame Street* puppeteers didn't know them either; they had never all been together.

Performing at Carnegie Hall was just such a blessing. It was never on my wish list. That year we were invited, as a cast, to be part of the Hollywood Bowl finale fireworks. The group Pink Martini closed the Hollywood Bowl season and they invited us to come and do a segment with a symphony orchestra. Hearing Jim's voice and hearing Joe's music played by a symphony was outstanding. The entrance to the stage of the Hollywood Bowl is quite a trip from the wings to center stage, and the show was sold out with 17,000 people singing the *Sesame Street* theme song. I know Joe—he must have really been smiling. With grownups singing it, I said, "This must be how rockers feel when the audience knows their song and sings it back to them." Carnegie Hall was above and beyond more than I could ever ask or think, and here's a part I adored. We didn't come out from the wings; they wanted us to come from the back of the house. We walked up the aisles and people hollered and screamed and touched our hands. I wore a red chiffon gold dress with big ring sleeves, and I held out my hands while I was coming up the aisle. It was fun. It was really fun.

On stage celebrating the musical world of Jim Henson at Carnegie Hall in 2012 with the cast and the New York Pops.

Even in my dreams as a kid, I never saw myself at Carnegie Hall or the Hollywood Bowl, but I used to take the cucumber and pretend it was a microphone. I saw myself singing on a stage in a big place. It felt like what my mother said to me just before she graduated to heaven, she said, "You're living your dream, aren't you baby?" And I said, "Yes ma'am, I am."

Recently Emilio Delgado reflected on how the performance at the Hollywood Bowl came together.

I had known the guys in Pink Martini. We met originally around 2007. They're based in Portland, Oregon. My wife Carol and I travel to Portland at least once or twice a year to visit her mom who lives there.

One of the times that we were there, we just happened to meet them. Once they figured out who I was, they asked me if I wanted to sing with them at a concert that they were doing in Portland. I agreed and I sang a couple of songs with them. That's where our friendship began.

Then before you knew it, they invited me to sing on one of their albums, so I sang, "Sing" with China Forbes, who is their female singer. She's fantastic, and I couldn't believe I was singing a duet with her on one of their albums. It was terrific.

The friendship just went like that. When they came to New York I sang with them a couple of times, once at Carnegie Hall of all places. I was singing at Carnegie Hall. I couldn't believe it.

In 2012 Paul Thomas Lauderdale called and he said,

"Emilio, you want to sing at the Hollywood Bowl with us?"

I said, "Yeah."

So the year before the whole Sesame Street cast performed there, I performed at the Hollywood Bowl with them as a solo act. I went there and I sang a couple of songs with them. I sang, "Sing," because that was on the album, and then I sang a Spanish song.

Then the year afterwards, they invited me back again. I said,

"Yeah, I'd love to do it."

Then Thomas called again later and he said,

"What if the whole cast of Sesame Street sang with us at the Hollywood Bowl?"

I said, "Let me call them. They're going to say yes."

That's when I called everybody and invited them to perform there with me.

Then we did three nights at the Hollywood Bowl, the whole cast, minus Linda who was in China and couldn't join us. You can imagine, we were just so—as they say in California—stoked. We were flying high.

The Hollywood Bowl holds thousands of people. It was so exciting. We weren't just singing with Pink Martini; we were singing with the symphony orchestra. When we entered the Hollywood Bowl, we entered from the wings and walked up to the stage. As we walked in, we were singing the show's theme song and the whole crowd was singing along. To hear all those people singing was amazing. It really was. The recognition was absolutely astounding. You can imagine what that feels like, when you walk out on stage and thousands of people already know you. It was truly amazing! That was quite an adventure that we had there and I'll never forget it.

Playing Gordon and Susan comes with a certain level of responsibility that we carried by being these symbols of love, harmony and respect. We are role models for parents and because of that our characters have been able to cover a wide range of topics over the years. Adoption was a topic that had never been approached before on the show. This was one of many other kinds of very difficult issues, or sensitive issues, that the show has covered, but this was one of the early ones. It was kick-started by the fact that I had a little baby boy, a bouncing baby boy, who would have been a perfect casting choice—my son, Miles. We decided to keep his name, Miles, on the show because he wouldn't answer to Joe or John. He did maybe four or five years or more on the show. At first it was really strange for him. Here was his dad—his real dad—that he was being the son of on the show, and here's this lady, Susan, who isn't his mom. It was a little confusing for him at first, but eventually he became a part of the Sesame Street *family just like everyone else. It was such a great experience for him, and for me as well, to share those years with him during his early development. Of course, getting to hang out in the Muppet room with those guys and hanging with his favorite characters all day wasn't a bad gig for a little toddler.*

Roscoe Orman, Gordon on Sesame Street, *1974-Present*

"SUSAN of Sesame St.
Loretta Long"

In this section of the book you'll find a collection of reflections written by viewers of **Sesame Street,** *my friends and my fellow cast mates. I collected these reflections over the last few years because I want to document the impact that this show and my portrayal of Susan has had on the audience.*

I hope you will enjoy reading them as much as I enjoyed collecting them.

Dr. Loretta Long

Part 6: Reflections

My earliest "Susan" memory has to be of the hurricane episode of **Sesame Street** *that I watched as a kid. Susan, Gordon and Miles were trying to take Big Bird's mind off the blackout and the hurricane by doing shadow puppets. That was always a warm scene for me. As I got older, I became a Muppet fan, which plunged me into studying classic* **Sesame Street** *clips. Susan did some of the best stuff for the show in the 70s. I've always enjoyed her line in "What's the Name of That Song" and another song from 1973 called "My Little Game." I bought the record of it and it's so catchy. But the best two songs she's probably ever sang were "Glop Grungy Glug Garden" with Oscar and "Picture a World" with Matt Robinson. That song is so soothing and makes you feel better about an otherwise cynical world.*

Melvin Campbell, Viewer

On the very cusp of my memory is the crush I had on Miss Susan.
She was so beautiful and kind, and I was naturally attracted to
her. Well, I lived in a white, middle-class neighborhood in the
early 70's. Racism was rampant in my neighborhood, but I didn't
understand it. My mother bought a **Sesame Street** *album for me*
and it was well played by me. Somehow I found out that Miss
Susan was coming to a local department store (Korvette's of Glen
Burnie, MD). I begged my mother and sister to take me to meet
Miss Susan. My sister, ten years my elder, took me to the
department store to meet Miss Susan despite my father's warnings
about taking me to see a black person. I'm sure it was more
colorfully said than that but I really don't remember those details.
I stood in line with a billion kids. I finally got my chance to step
up to Miss Susan for her autograph of my **Sesame Street** *album.*
She gave me a kiss and I swear I almost fainted. This was my first
bout with racism. I thought it was deplorable that my father was
so against me going to meet someone because of their skin color.
I believe that moment molded my beliefs that racism was wrong.
From that moment on, I began my fight against racism by
example. To this day it is still a battle unfortunately, but I think
we're winning. Miss Susan, thanks so much for the influence you
have given to my life. I'll always remember you!

Steve Michalek, Baltimore, MD

I grew up on a multicultural street in the Richmond Hill section of Queens, NY in the 1980s watching **Sesame Street** *daily on our television set with a dial (no remote) and encased in wood. Seeing all of the people from different backgrounds live happily together was how my friends and I were molded and shown how to act when the television was off and we were outside playing. There weren't any racial fights and no put-downs. We shared our cultures and our family values with one another. When I think of Gordon and Susan, I think of the couple that were the moral compass of both* **Sesame Street** *and our lives. Susan was always nurturing, kind, compassionate, and understanding. Now, at the age of thirty-five, I am experiencing Gordon, Susan, and the entire* **Sesame Street** *experience again with my one-year-old daughter. What an exhilarating thrill to be connected across time through that special street full of monsters and wonderful people from all different backgrounds! When I think back on* **Sesame Street,** *I think that my utmost favorite memory of Susan is when she is singing "True Blue Miracle" with Olivia, looking up into the tree and teaching us young people what was so magical about Christmas. I recently watched it with my daughter and I could not help the tears that filled my eyes. It was like walking down that old familiar block from long ago, seeing old friends, and singing the old songs that you sang together.*

Susan was always cheerful, never cross, and could even make Oscar's cantankerous behavior be subdued. And how would Big Bird have gotten along without her? I can guarantee that every child dreams of sitting on the front stoop of 1-2-3 Sesame Street or meeting Susan, Gordon and everyone else. How fortunate that thirty-five years later technology has not just left this a dream, but now a reality. I hope that Sesame Street *always remains and that my dear friends from long ago continue to teach harmony. I do not like the word tolerance. Tolerance to me is just restraining hatred. Harmony is the love in your heart for the person, regardless of the color or creed. Thank you, Loretta Long for dedicating your life to all of us kids as Susan!*

Peter Franzese, Viewer

When I was six, my mother took me to a big store to meet
Susan. To a six year old in 1970, Susan didn't need a last name;
I don't think she even had one. The show was **Sesame Street,**
and this was Susan.

As my mom and I stood in the long line, my expectations got very
low, because I was remembering what happened last year. Last
year, we had stood in a line like this one to meet Bob McAllister
from Wonderama. I remembered him as not looking at all like he
did on TV, and being cold and unfriendly. In retrospect, this was
unfair to Mr. McAllister. As a five year old, I had expected him to
look exactly the same as he did on television, including being
small and in washed out color. Also, he had been dealing with
children all day, signing copies of his album, and I stood in front
of him.

Bob McAllister: Hi, what's your name?
Me [shyly]: Doug. [pause][signs album]
Bob McAllister: Here you are.

I hadn't given him a lot to work with, and there were many, many,
children to get through.

So, expectations lowered, I mentally rehearsed my question for

Susan. I had loved **Sesame Street** *from the first year it had been broadcast and was ready for the logical next step, but that next step hadn't come. So I was going to ask Susan, "Why don't they have* **Sesame Street** *stuff in cereal boxes?" I had never questioned the progression: Hit Show - - > Cereal Box Toy. Except for* **Sesame Street.** *The world was not working as the world worked. And I rehearsed and rehearsed. "Why don't they have* **Sesame Street** *stuff in cereal boxes?" "Why don't they have* **Sesame Street** *stuff in cereal boxes?"*

And then we came to Susan. And it turned out that Susan was the most beautiful woman I had ever seen, except for Mommy. I have a poor visual memory but here I am, over forty years later, with a distinct memory of how she looked with stacks of copies her new album in front of her and a blurry store behind her. She had the kind of presence that just radiated. I couldn't talk, I just stared. She was so, so, pretty in real life, even more than she was on **Sesame Street.** *And her voice when she said, "Hi, what's your name?" sounded just like it did on TV. She was Susan.*

You know, making fun of the clichéd "Peace and Love" part of the late 60s/early 70s is so established that it is also a cliché. But those of us who were around, even as little children, will tell you that there was something there. Maybe not what it was marketed

168

to be, maybe not what it was claimed to be, but there was something. Susan exuded that magic. I'm sure even the grownups in that store that day noticed it. As a child, I experienced it as almost a tangible thing. I remember thinking, "I can feel her smile." Take away the 60s trappings, the tie-dye and drugs and beads and long hair, boil it all away until you just get that pure Love, that "All you need is" Love. That Love was all around her that day. And I felt it flow from her into me as she signed my album with a line of children behind me. I didn't walk away after she handed me my signed copy of "Susan Sings Songs from Sesame Street.*" I had a question.*

"Why don't they have Sesame Street *things in cereal boxes?" Last minute change to remove the slang. Susan gave me complete 100% attention while I asked and didn't talk down to me when she answered. That matters a lot to a bright six year old. Most strangers talked down to me. But then again, this wasn't really a stranger, it was Susan. "Oh! That's an excellent question. You see,* Sesame Street *gets its money from the government, while other television shows get their money from advertisers, and there is a grant..." I don't remember everything, and it started to go over my head. Hers too, because I have another distinct visual memory – of Susan rolling her eyes while lifting her head and waving her hand in the air, "...I don't understand it all myself." She made sympathetic eye contact with*

my mom at that point, the first time she took her eyes off of me. But she explained to me that this was why I would never see **Sesame Street** *toys in cereal boxes, and that there would never be* **Sesame Street** *dolls or toys or clothing or anything like that. And I was okay with it. (And another visual memory – this one that I haven't thought of in over forty years – I just found a photo in a mental photo album that I didn't know existed – I see Susan's face and extended hand right before we shook hands and said goodbye.)*

I assumed, because I knew how the world worked, that next year we would meet Gordon to buy his album, and then Bob the next year, and Mr. Hooper the year after that. People took turns. That didn't happen, of course, but lots of other stuff did, and here I am. I don't talk down to children. That bothers some and gladdens others. Did I learn that just from Susan? No, my twelve-year-older brother Mike never talked down to me, and my other siblings and parents often didn't. But those few minutes with Susan are such an important memory, and I can't separate who I am from those few minutes – they are an integral ingredient in the stew, the stuff – no, the Things That Have Happened. It would have been so easy for her to dismiss my question. "Because Oscar doesn't like cereal," said with a smile and an implied "Next!" But she took the time and I will be

always grateful to her. Loretta Long. I didn't know that at the
time, but I wanted to thank her by name. Thank you, Loretta
Long.

Dr. Doug Shaw, University of Northern Iowa

I'm one of the Muppeteers. I came here to the United States twenty-five years ago. I'm originally from Mexico, and in Mexico we have **Plaza Sésamo.** *It's not like the* **Sesame Street** *here. We have our own street with our own human actors, and so when I came here it was the first time that I was introduced to everybody in the cast. My experience with Loretta was incredible because I came here and my English was very, very, very limited. I do remember the people in the cast—they were warm and caring and helpful, and Loretta was one of them who stood out to me. I remember she told me that when she started* **Sesame Street,** *there were no people of color on TV.*

Loretta said that I should, "Hang in there."

She said that since I was from Mexico that just meant that I was going to be an example for other Latino kids. She gave me strength. It was amazing.

I was just very happy to have somebody like her around when I came to work on **Sesame Street.**

Carmen Osbahr, Rosita on **Sesame Street,** *1989-present*

I am so happy to have this opportunity to remember this wonderful fact about Loretta Long, who plays Susan on **Sesame Street.**

I was very much impressed by Loretta/Susan way before I met her. I saw her on television at my university. I was attending Carnegie-Mellon University in Pittsburgh, and I remember walking into the student union and there on the screen was a very young, very bald James Earl Jones reciting the alphabet in a very deliberate manner ... A ... B ... C ... while the letters flashed over his head.

It was such a compelling image; I actually thought I was watching a show that taught lip-reading. But the best was yet to come because, when they cut to the street and I saw Loretta Long playing Susan, I was knocked off my feet. I had never seen such a cheerful, beautiful African American person talking to me from an environment that was very much like my own.

She and Matt Robinson, who played Gordon her husband on the show at that time, were this lovely American-as-apple-pie couple talking to children from the inner city. They were cheerful, and wonderful, and warm and loving.

It's very hard for me and for many to get this across, but in 1969 there were no people of color on television. You'd be shocked when you saw a person of color on television, and if you did they certainly weren't this beautiful, warm, friendly couple that was so nurturing.

That was the first glimpse that I had of Loretta Long playing Susan on Sesame Street, and it is branded in my brain and I will never forget it. I thank her for being that person.

Sonia Manzano, Maria on Sesame Street, 1974-2015

Before I was on **Sesame Street**, *I had all the LPs and would put them on in my room, close the door, take my brush, and turn it upside down and sing, "With You." I would sing, "Some day little children, some day soon," and I'd do all the parts... "Some day soon there's gonna be a lot of people" over and over.*

The first year I was on the show I couldn't believe it. I was just so star struck by everyone, including Loretta. I was very, very intimidated by her presence, how she carried herself. It amazed me. There were so many different aspects of meeting Loretta because I was meeting a childhood idol that I already felt like I knew deeply. These characters and the cast meant the world to me. For any child who has any havoc in their life, **Sesame Street** *at that time really symbolized a sense of comfort and peace. All the cast members like Susan and Gordon really were family to me before I ever set foot on the set.*

The way in which Loretta Long carries herself is so poignant and beautiful to me, and it always has been. I made sure, as a fifteen year old to really, really stay in shape when I was around her, because I really wanted her respect; I really did. It was so obvious that she had fought hard to get where she was.

When I say I was intimidated when I met her it was more like,

"Shut up and listen. Shut up and listen. Shut up and listen."

When I was 15, 16, 17, I struggled a lot with anxiety. I had terrible anxiety. I was in the makeup room one day in Lee Halls' chair, and Loretta said,

"You okay?"

I remember saying, "Yeah. I think I'm just feeling a little anxiety."

Loretta was so beautiful and graceful. She talked me through it. She told me what helps her. She said,

"The mean voices aren't God."

She also gave me tapes, like self-help tapes, that I would listen to by myself. They were very spiritual and there was a very healing undertone to them. From that day, I understood where she came from. She came from that place of God, her belief, her faith. I will never forget that. She was so nice to me during those jittery years of trying to figure everything out. I thank her with all of my heart. Thank you Loretta Long.

Allison Bartlett O'Reilly, Gina on Sesame Street, *1987-Present*

It was extraordinary working with Loretta and with all these people. Here I was a young actor just starting out. At that point I had only done this repertory stuff and had done a bunch of acting workshops. I hadn't done any television yet at that time.

I had worked with all kinds of people, but working on **Sesame Street** *with Loretta and with all of the other people that were on the show—it was just so amazing. I was blown away that all these people on the show were so friendly.*

It was like a family situation. We worked so well together. It was like we'd just do a scene like we had done it before. It was so amazing to be working with all these people.

By the time **Sesame Street** *became a reality for me, Loretta had already been on the show for a couple of years along with Bob. When I arrived, they just took me in.*

It was like they were saying,

"Where have you been? Welcome back."

It was like you hit the ground running with these people. That was an awesome feeling.

I remember the first scene that I ever did was with Big Bird. I was so nervous, my knees were shaking. We got on the set and the cameras were rolling. Jon Stone was directing and the first lines came up. Right off the bat, I goofed a line.

Caroll said to me, "Just relax. Just play with it," or something like that. That put me at ease a little bit and, from then on, it was easy as pie.

Every time that I was on the set with Loretta, Bob and Caroll and all the people that came afterwards, it was like being in a family. I can say that we're related. Loretta and I are brother and sister.

I think that feeling also comes from all of those good times with Loretta when we were all singing all those numbers together like, "What's the Name of That Song?" The songs have become iconic and, just as the audience will never forget those songs, I'll never forget performing them with Loretta and all of the other cast members.

Emilo Delgado, Luis on **Sesame Street, 1971-present**

I was born in 1966, so at three years old when **Sesame Street** *took off, I was a member of the targeted audience. My memories of* **Sesame Street** *are wonderful ones. I truly believe that this show taught me not only the alphabet, small words, Spanish, numbers, simple math and problem solving, but it prepared me for kindergarten where I would be exposed to people of color. I always thought that Susan was such a lovely character and she made me feel so loved and important. I thought she was beautiful. When I went to a school where there were a few black kids in my class, I admired their beauty and never saw anything beyond the fact that their color was darker than mine. My mom and dad bought me a* **Sesame Street** *album that featured Susan and other cast members. I loved singing with her! I can remember one of my favorite episodes about the number 2 and Susan singing it with Bob. My favorite clip about the number 2 with the dollhouse, two little girls and two cats crashing a tea party is a treasured memory! What a memory. I've looked that up on YouTube a few times to share with my own kids and as a reminder to my peers. I had the honor and privilege of meeting Dr. Loretta Long (Susan) in person when I recognized her on a city street. I was so excited to talk to her and she looked into my eyes and held my hands and made me feel so special. Standing there I felt three again at 47.*

Linda McKenna, Viewer

I'm a 28-year-old fan of **Sesame Street** *from The Netherlands. It's called* **Sesamstraat** *over here and the Dutch version of the show started in 1976. The original songs were overdubbed with Dutch lyrics and there was also a lot of original material. So, I have never seen you as Susan until YouTube started coming along—way, way past my childhood.*

However, my parents bought the first "Sesame Street Book & Record" as an import. I have no idea why. Your great voice is present on this LP and we loved those songs. Now that I'm a father myself, I keep coming back to those songs to sing for my own son. With all the online streaming services one can hear the whole back catalog that wasn't issued in my country. Unbelievable how many great LPs were recorded while you all were also making a great TV show.

I think a historian should dive into the writers (Joe Raposo, Jeff Moss come to mind), musicians and singers who made these incredible records. I would love to read about your thoughts about recording those songs. Songs that surely made an impact overseas.

Jop Euwijk, Dutch historian

I was seven years old when **Sesame Street** *debuted on WTTW Channel 11 out of Chicago and Loretta Long (pre Dr.) came into my living room for the first time. Being a gay man and having grown up in a small community, I totally understand the importance of diversity and have admired Dr. Long's work for many years (both onscreen and off). She was an inspiration to me as a young boy who grew up during the Civil Rights Movement and the days of Martin Luther King Jr. in the mid-60s.* **Dr. Loretta Long** *and* **Sesame Street** *have long had an impact on my life and the pride I have in celebrating my part in our diverse culture! I loved her then in 1969 and I love and respect her now in 2013! She continues to be a very classy lady and a pioneer in Children's Television. I wish her the best now and in her future projects and endeavors. She is a wonderful human being whether she is 'Susan' or Dr. Loretta Long. All my best to you Dr. Long! Thank you for being a part of my childhood and an inspiration on into my adult years. You are a blessing to many! Keep on keeping on!*

With Much Love and Admiration,

Todd Wathen

When I was a toddler (about two or three years of age), my mother would sit me down in front of the television so that I could watch Sesame Street. By the time I reached the start of my school years, I was deemed to be an advanced student. I know now that I owe this largely to Sesame Street, as it was a staple in my daily activities—a fundamental building block in the base of my education. Seeing Susan, an African-American woman, living on a block that looked like mine, portrayed in a positive manner made me feel comfortable. It was like spending time with a friendly aunt. The fact that there were so many other races (and when it came to the Muppets, colors) represented in one neighborhood helped me learn that we are all more alike on the inside than we are different on the outside.

As an adult I reminisced with my mother about the show. Before she passed, she told me that her insistence that I watch Sesame Street was more than just for entertainment purposes. My late mother was a very smart woman. She came from a very small town in rural North Carolina and felt that there were certain limitations to the formal education she had received. Knowing that there were a number of things that she would not be well equipped to teach me, she was savvy enough to find a learning resource that would be complimentary to the life lessons she

182

would bestow upon me. As a parent now myself, I have passed down the tradition of learning through engagement and fun to my own daughter. I am sure that **Sesame Street,** *with its endearing characters and universal lessons will be around for many generations to come.*

James Miller, Musician, age 37

My father was in the military, stationed in Germany. That is where I was born and spent the first two years of my life. Everything that I knew of American culture came from my family and the VHS tapes that were shipped to us by loved ones. Among those tapes: **Sesame Street.**

Sesame Street *helped me learn the basics, letters, numbers, counting. It was both fun and educational. The various cultures represented helped me learn about people living together even though they have differences. While I did not come from a multi-cultured home, this was still very helpful to me as an American living in Germany.*

Looking back now, pregnant with my own multi-cultured child, I realize that those lessons carried forward into my adult life. We are different. We are many. We are one. Now, if only Susan and Oscar had taught a lesson on how to get along with your mother-in-law.....

Cassie Kokes, age 22, expecting mother

The theme song of **Sesame Street** *was like the "pied piper" for my daughter. She was introduced to this show as soon as she came home from the hospital in the late 70s, and I watched the progression of her devotion over the preschool years. It started with simply turning her head on the bed toward that music. This progressed to rolling over for a better view, and as she got older sitting in her high chair and responding to what was going on by banging on the tray. If anyone, or anything, blocked her view she would definitely let you know. By the time she progressed to sitting on the floor in front of the television, she knew the characters and was very much involved in the lessons that were taught on each episode. Other than the excellent content of the show, I also credit* **Sesame Street** *with something else. She knew that it was time for her program (*Sesame Street*) and when I did not come fast enough to turn the television on and put it on the right channel, she decided that she was capable of doing this herself! This was another* **Sesame Street** Life Lesson *in my household.*

From my perspective, other than the theme song, which is unforgettable, I was very much impressed with the way Susan interacted with the children on the show. When working with children, I'm sure that there were times when a child (or the children) did not react to a situation in the way that had been planned. With Susan's interpersonal skills she always made the situation/lesson work regardless. Also, the whole integrated cast (the adults and the children) was a big plus for me!!! This was unheard of in the seventies, and it made a huge impression on me! Sesame Street *was ahead of its time in many ways.*

Europa Gay, 71, Entrepreneur, DoD-DLA (Retired)

I think that the minute you heard "Sunny days..." in the theme song you were excited to sit down and watch another episode of **Sesame Street.** *Growing up in the cultural melting pot of Queens, New York, I had neighbors of different backgrounds.* **Sesame Street** *represented this with people who were Black, Brown and White. The people of color on the show provided positive images, which were lacking in many other shows at that time.*

In addition to a wonderful amount of diversity, **Sesame Street** *taught you how to spell, read and count in a fun manner. I still remember singing "I'm a baby ga ga goo goo rocka rocka" or doing numbers with* **The Count.**

I'm glad that my little cousins and friends' children have been given the same opportunity to watch a show that was truly ahead of its time!

Alyson Myers, 36, Endocrinologist

Assistant Professor, Hofstra Medical School

Sesame Street has been a building block of culture for my entire life. Some of my first memories involve the indelible characters of the show, most prominently Big Bird, the overgrown avian with a childlike wonder that we all wish we could retain beyond our youth. The show gave me a sense that the rest of the world beyond my hometown of East Harlem, USA, might also look like my friends and family. People in various shades of brown, tan, and cream were not just teaching me the alphabet...they were interacting with my yellow-feathered, blue, and red heroes!

Susan Robinson was one of these people, a beautiful brown-skinned woman with a welcoming and engaging smile as portrayed by Dr. Loretta Long. Her character and the entire cast have stayed with me for the greater part of my life, first in the forefront of my toddler brain, and then eventually fading into the background (as longtime family friends sometimes do) as I got older and grew into a man. The best thing about Sesame Street *is that, in my mind, it has always been there.*

Three years ago when my wife and I had our son, Austin, there was no question that we would eventually expose him to the same cast of characters that our own parents had first shown us over three decades ago now. Not surprisingly, most mornings you can find him at the dining table, eating his breakfast while marveling over the entertaining antics of monsters, animals, and people that he now thinks of as his friends. I make sure to remind him occasionally that they belonged to me first.

Loren Hammonds, 37, Director, Sales & Operations, Tribeca Cinemas; Musician

What I liked about **Sesame Street** *as a child was the playful and colorful characters and puppets. As a child, I didn't see the show as teaching me something.* **Sesame Street** *was a show that entertained me.*

Not until I was older and aged out of the program did I recognize all the important themes that the show conveyed to young children. The various ethnicities portrayed on the show spoke volumes: no matter how different we think we all are, we share many of the same basic values.

Growing up in the Bronx, most folks in my community looked like me. We were either African-American or Latino. **Sesame Street** *blended kids of all races together and let us know we can play and be in harmony with each other – we like the same things. Those who are different from me still like what I like. As a kid, establishing that common ground is essential in developing relationships.*

Kareen Bell, 42, Finance Specialist, Coca-Cola
Lifetime Member, Delta Sigma Theta, Inc.

I am a "multiculti." My parents, being foreigners (each from a different country than the other), never watched **Sesame Street.** *My sister, Kyla, and I were first gen watchers. It had a big impact on my childhood, like most people I know. In fact, Oscar was my favorite puppet—which my friends might say explains my lovable demeanor now.*

The omnipresent rainbow of diversity created by the cast and puppets and Muppets on **Sesame Street** *always reinforced the lessons that I learned at home:*

- Being different makes you unique.

- Being unique makes you extraordinary.

- Extraordinary is never bad!

I think my mother, especially, knew the importance and value of having the option of leaving us (individually as it were) in front of the TV with a bowl of cereal to watch something educational and engaging. And, it was on PBS—my folks fervently supported NYC's Channel 13! It also meant a little more sleep for her in the morning. When it came to **Sesame Street,** *she must've really trusted the "people in my neighborhood!"*

Dave Kupferstein, 37, Musician and GastroArtisan

As a young child, you could do no better in my book than by tuning in to **Sesame Street.** *I saw "Sesame Street Live," I had a subscription to the publication, I had books, I had dolls, I had an Ernie radio (and a rubber ducky), I had countless albums, and the list goes on and on. The multi-ethnic, uber-colorful format felt right to me. Although one cannot tell from my appearance, I came from a multi-cultured home.*

My late father was from Nigeria, my mother is an African-American from small town North Carolina...and I was being raised as a city kid in New York. We were the only black family on our block, the parents of the house next door were from Spain, the next house had a Jewish family, and in the next beyond them was an Asian family. Because of the specialized schools that I attended, my friends have always come from different neighborhoods, different socio-economic backgrounds and different (often multiple) ethnicities. My mother, like those that Jim Henson surrounded himself with, saw the importance of diversity early on.

Seeing Susan Robinson (played by Dr. Loretta Long) reinforced the image of the strong, African-American female role model that I had in my mother. Susan and my mother (with the help of the community of mothers that I was blessed to have in my life) taught me that there was no shame in looking different than

*others, that there was nothing wrong with being a "smart girl,"
that I could be whatever I wanted to be in life, and (most
importantly) to always act and react with kindness.*

As I grew, so did my love of all things "Henson": **The Muppet
Show, The Muppet Babies** *cartoon,* **Fraggle Rock** *(we didn't
have cable during the early years, so my mother had a co-worker
make VHS recordings for me that I still have). And then there
were the numerous Muppet movies. As a child, I went to see them
in the theater and, as an adult-aged child, I now own them on
VHS and DVD—you can never have too many back-ups.*

Now I watch **Sesame Street** *with my Godchildren. The second
youngest, Dayanara, started kindergarten last week. I have no
doubt that Day is well-armed for success—carrying with her the
knowledge and wisdom of Susan and all of my lifelong friends in
her neighborhood.*

*The conceptual brilliance of Henson in making all of the Muppets
different colors (even within the same family) was
groundbreaking!* **Sesame Street** *was, and is, a shining example of
the utopian society that each generation strives nearer to still.*

*Ariadne DeGarr-Miller, 37, Faithful Neighborhood Dweller since
'77*

I have two children of my own who watched (and continue to watch) the show. My youngest daughter is five years old. I remember one day, several years ago, while I was channel surfing how excited she got about one of the channels that I'd sped past. When I turned back, I saw that it was **Sesame Street.** *It didn't matter what else was going on in my home, she had heard Elmo's voice and her eyes were now peeled to the show. Elmo was our "in." She was hooked on what she thought was a new discovery. Elmo introduced her to a whole new group of friends and "neighbors." After that, she was learning in no time while thinking it was all just fun and games and songs.*

Every year that followed, every birthday, every Christmas, our friends and family members were buying her something "Sesame Street"—books, toys, DVDs. I even bought the "40 Years of Sunny Days" DVD for us to watch as a family. In fact, she's watching it right now as I write this. The more we watched, the more familiar memories came back to me. Skits I didn't realize that I knew, melodies that were all too familiar. The interactive teaching styles of **Sesame Street** *even inspire my approach to education in my own classroom. It's a great way for the whole family to connect and share lessons that have meant so much to all of us at some point in our lives.*

Natasha Plair, Early Childhood Education Specialist

Saying that my brother and I remember watching Sesame Street *when we were children would be imprecise. It would be like saying that we remember living in our home.* Sesame Street *was not a television program that we enjoyed from time to time, it was a steady presence that enveloped us from our earliest moments and that has stayed with us always.* Sesame Street *pervaded completely our most formative years. It cultivated our sensibilities. It molded our personalities. The language* of Sesame Street *was assimilated so thoroughly into our own that today we do not identify certain turns of phrase as being borrowed from* Sesame Street *because they have become integrally ours.* Sesame Street *was our introduction to entertainment and the impact that this early and constant exposure had on our future interpretations of cultural works is immeasurable. In the ninth grade I was outraged that O. Henry's short story "The Gift of the Magi" had blatantly plagiarized Ernie and Bert's heartbreaking exchange in "Christmas Eve on* Sesame Street.*" My brother has always resented The Beatles for stealing "Letter B" and he has never forgiven Bruce Springsteen for poaching "Born to Add." For us, Sherlock Hemlock and Cyranose De Bergerac are the genuine article, and not those other characters whose acquaintance we made later on. "Christmas Eve on* Sesame Street*" is of special significance to my brother and me. We did not watch it only at Christmas time. As Bob and Linda's song prescribed, we kept Christmas with us all through the year. If we were not watching it* *on video, we were listening to the audiocassette. When my brother was older, he played that cassette when he had trouble falling asleep. At 31 and 27 years old we still watch "Christmas Eve on Sesame Street" when we are together at Christmas, at least once, and throughout the year it echoes in our every interaction. We recite and reenact it, often without thinking.*

When we met Dr. Loretta Long in August of 2014, she was as kind and as gracious as we could ever have hoped the real life Susan to be.

As we walked away from her, Peter turned to me and said,

"And if that isn't a true, blue miracle…"

We finished together,

"I don't know what one is."

My brother and I do not remember that we watched Sesame Street *when we were children. We remember that* Sesame Street *was our childhood.*

Lori and Peter Mele

In the early 1980's, I was a young mother of three children under the age of five. I was proud that had earned a master in education but felt petrified and unprepared because I had never taken a single class in parenting. What a daunting task! Each day was overwhelming. I started my mornings with devotion and prayer along with that special cup of coffee before my silence was broken by the pitter-patter of little feet. My philosophy was that tomorrow was never promised and that I must instill all I can in my children each day. My ancestors had instilled within me the value of a good education. I trusted and relied on it to take me to endless caverns that emptied into pools of solutions. My graduate training taught me the necessity of measurable goals, objectives, review, pretest, and posttest strategies within curriculum. I created an early education curriculum worthy of doctoral dissertation. I really was ahead of my time.

I loved, no LOVED, Sesame Street! We watched it each morning and afternoon on KCET, the Public Broadcasting Station in Los Angeles. I had a white board in my kitchen and on it we would write the number, letter, and word of the day. Throughout the day we spied street signs or house numbers or newspapers that contained these daily elements. Grocery stores were a treasure trove of opportunities for reinforcement. There were countless example of greens and yellows and reds right in the produce

section. The girls learned about international foods like bok choy,
mango, and hummus. Even doing the laundry became a teaching
opportunity. We sang the song "Three of these things belong
together but one of these things doesn't belong here" to reinforce
our daily learning. I wanted their learning to be fun and I knew it
needed to incorporate multiple intelligence of dancing and
singing, visual special memory, as well as sharpening of auditory
memory.

At the end of our busy day, while preparing dinner, we watched
the afternoon program, which was exactly the same as the
morning program. It reinforced what we had been learning
throughout the day. Did we have a library of **Sesame Street**
videos, books, and dolls? Absolutely! I also credit **Sesame Street**
for introducing my children to multiple languages, new cultures,
acceptance of similarities over differences, and emotional
intelligence. It was Kermit singing "It's Not Easy Being Green"
that helped one child deal with peer rejection due to her race. It
was Big Bird who taught them that childhood grief and loss are a
very confusing time. Big Bird represented the little child in all of
us. We all had to wrap our minds around the fact that death is a
part of life. No Big Bird, Mr. Looper {that's Hooper} was not
coming back. We eventually must learn to let the memories
reshape us. Death and loss change us, and so does divorce.

Today, these three children are grown women. They became

National Honor Society members, notables in **Who's Who in American High School Students,** *and NCAA Academic All Americans. Their scholastic achievements earned college scholarships to elite colleges from which they have all matriculated. They are well-rounded women who have found love in the eyes of partners from international countries. I credit part of that to those early days of prayer, a good cup of coffee, and to* **Sesame Street.**

Lela C. Hairston

Right away Loretta and I understood each other, which was great. We just hit it off as friends. Sesame Street *was a new thing for everybody because it was a different kind of show. We hit it off as friends, which I always get a big kick out of because I was in a stupid clown show before that and I doubt I did anything that was particularly intelligent. I felt I could, but you don't do that on the* Bozo Show. *It was such a great experience to work with such great actors and singers like Loretta and everyone else. Back then Matt Robinson played Gordon; he was a brilliant guy to work*

with. He was fun. I remember the three of us having lots of fun in the kitchen of the house on 1-2-3 Sesame Street. There was one time we were held up there for such a long time. In the early years of the show, we had such technical problems that sometimes short scenes could take hours to shoot. Somehow Loretta just found a way to make it fun.

When I think about the longevity that she, Bob and I have had in these roles, it's just really great. I'm so glad that it doesn't have to stop. I have decided that I'm just going to stay with this show as long as they want me. It's hard to believe but it has already been 45 years.

It's really a physically demanding job to be Big Bird. I would be in the suit and then have to climb into the trashcan when the rest of the cast would go back to their dressing rooms. Sometimes, when I would get out of that suit I would think,

Wow, how many years can I do this?

When I asked Jim Henson (he's the person who hired me) what I would get paid to play Big Bird he said,

"Well we have a tradition."

I said, "I like traditions."

He said, "Oh you won't like this one."

I said, "Why?"

He said, "You won't get paid much."

I said, "Oh I thought I was going to get bloody rich." Then we both laughed. After that, I found out that children who would come on the show, they were getting better pay than I did. They said puppeteers don't get paid a lot and they proved it. I took a big pay cut to take this job but it eventually worked out for me. It worked out for all of us and I am so happy I took the job because if I hadn't, I may have never met my dear friend Loretta Long.

Caroll Spinney, Big Bird and Oscar the Grouch,
1969-Present

I was one of the people that actually grew up with the original cast I used to watch all of the time when I was a child. On my very first day on the **Sesame Street** *set I was very nervous and I walked into the wardrobe room and Loretta was standing there and she introduced herself to me.*

She said, " How old are you?"

I told her my age.

She said, "I raised you, come here."

Then she gave me a big hug. I was like she's absolutely right, she did raise me. It really made me feel at ease knowing that I was with family on my very first day on the show. It was such a great memory and I tell that story all of the time.

Alan Muraoka, Alan of the Sesame Street *cast, 1998-Present*

Growing up, I loved the movie "Follow That Bird." There was just something about the movie that I could never get enough of. When I saw Sesame Street when I was young, I knew immediately that I had to be there because of the warmth and the humanity that was happening on screen. Oh, and I loved the crazy monsters. That's what it felt like in my head as a kid within my imagination. When I got there, everybody was exactly like they were on Sesame Street in real life—warm, embracing, immediately family and welcoming, I just couldn't believe it.

I guess the best thing about watching the show as a kid and then growing up and being part of the show as an adult was that when I meet the people I watched over all those years, I wanted them to be exactly like who they are on screen. Loretta is exactly like who she is on television and it's just so magical.

Leslie Carrara Rudolph, Puppeteer, Abby Cadabby, 2006-Present

When I met Loretta during our wonderful stint in the 1967 Music Fair Professional Summer Stock productions of "Milk and Honey" starring Molly Picon, Earl Wrightson and Lois Hunt and "Guys and Dolls" starring the iconic Betty Grable as "Adelaide," I was a sheltered, naïve teen of 18. I remember immediately connecting with her caring spirit and infectious personality. As a young adult, several years her junior, I looked up to Loretta as a mentor. She was so caring and always filled a room with light and love—just by being Loretta. I have always felt truly blessed to have known her and especially to call her my friend.

When Loretta initially contacted me to share her new Sesame Street endeavor and how—for the first time—preschoolers would

have the opportunity to learn and grow through a

fun and innovative, groundbreaking TV program, I was

impressed, but not surprised. Knowing Loretta's dedication to

education, as well as her talent and background in entertainment,

I felt it was the perfect fit for her.

In the 60s we were both passionate about singing and

dancing professionally. But while Loretta was pursuing her

Sesame Street dreams in the 70s, I was just beginning my

undergraduate education major, followed by medical school,

leading to community education of vital medical issues as the

health reporter on the NBC-TV News affiliate in Philadelphia

during my post-grad medical training in the mid-late 70s. In the

80s I continued at NBC in Phoenix, AZ and USA Cable, and

then formed my own company in 1985 to produce award-winning

video and workbook prevention/education curricula for 4-12

grades (currently distributed by Discovery Education). It is quite

serendipitous that after our musical theater connection, our lives

took on similar paths as teachers and role models for young

people throughout the past forty years.

I am so proud of Loretta's accomplishments; she is a true

trailblazer. Not only has she become a Sesame Street

icon, Loretta is a shining star for millions of youth who watched

her kind, nurturing ways each day on television for decades—and
still do!

While Loretta was busy with her growing **Sesame Street** *duties in*
the 70s and I continued on with my medical studies and career,
plus a growing family, we lost track of each other. However, our
joyous memories together in musical theater were always
treasured. Throughout the 70s and 80s, I watched Loretta and
shared the valuable lessons on **Sesame Street** *with our own*
children. We even attended their local events in hopes of
seeing her again. Alas, it wasn't to be until, thanks to social
media, I was able to track her down and reconnect just this past
year. A joyous reunion indeed! Loretta's beautiful smile and
energy are brighter than ever, and so is our special
friendship. There are very few people in the entertainment field
who have had such a profound impact on young people as
Loretta. Not only in giving children from intercity areas a stellar
role model to look up to and emulate, but her comforting,
nurturing persona shined through in each scene, touching every
viewer with sincerity and kindness that is Loretta Long.

Lynne D. Kitei, M.D.

(Top) In the cast of "Guys and Dolls" with Dr. Lynne Kitei 1968.

(Bottom) With Dr. Lynne Kitei summer 2014.

Who doesn't love Susan? It's hard to articulate how someone helps you form values and viewpoints as a child. As an adult you can articulate it much better. As a child, whatever you view you absorb. That's why I think ages 0 - 5 are so critical because that's when you just absorb everything. You don't even know what you're absorbing then.

Susan on **Sesame Street** *was just a part of my childhood. She came to Belvedere Mall and I got to meet her when I was about eleven years old. It was an unforgettable experience.*

I was born in 1970 and was watching the show at a very early age, not too long after it premiered on PBS.

When I was a child, my father worked first shift and my mother worked third shift. As my mother got home from work, my father was going off to work. While my parents worked and slept, I spent a lot of time with my sister and the television kept us company. My mother would fall asleep and leave PBS on for me. At that time, PBS was the only safe channel for children. I often watched Sesame Street *and that's how I got to know all of the characters. That's also how I got to know Susan.*

Sesame Street *was always very much a part of us growing up because we didn't have the options we have now. There was no internet. My parents were strict about what we could watch on TV and PBS was really a mainstay for us.*

When I met Susan, it was magical. It was magical in the sense that she was the first celebrity that I had ever met and she was so warm. I didn't expect anything other than Susan at that age. It wasn't until I became an adult that I realized the people you see on TV are not always really like the people they play. However, Loretta Long was really like Susan. She was pretty and her makeup was done so beautifully. I couldn't believe I was meeting her. As I grew up, I have always cherished a photo of the two of us together that was taken that day.

As an adult I lived overseas in Korea and we didn't have a lot of television channels to watch. But we did have the Military Channel, which showed older **Sesame Street** *episodes. For me that was comforting because it took me back to that time and that space of when I was a child. To see the people on television from home, which meant so much to me as a child, made me feel like I had my home right around me again.*

When I was growing up, Loretta Long was very much the fabric of many young girls' lives. I would have to say, being a black woman, she was pretty much a super star to me. I didn't get to see people like her on TV. I am so happy that she was part of my childhood and I am so grateful to able to say that I had the chance to meet her.

Marian L. Fortner, Ed.D

As a parent you never really discuss things that are very tough with your children when they're young. You sort of just make them do things. What I did when I was parenting my children was I showed television shows that I watched as a child that helped me learn so many valuable lessons. I spent a lot of money and a lot of time buying everything that I grew up with on DVD so I could show the programs to my kids. Sesame Street was one of those series that I bought to watch with them because I just loved the show as a child. The cartoons and television shows that entertain kids now are totally different than what entertained us. When you become a parent you lose sight of that. All you know is: I'm going to teach my kid and show my kid what I grew up on. I think that's because we always are thinking things like, the last time I checked I turned out okay, so they're going to turn out okay. My kids took to Sesame Street. They watched the episodes and enjoyed it. I'm going to be honest, they weren't as big of a fan as I was, but they were entertained and enjoyed the show very much. They would talk about it and they loved Big Bird, Ernie and Bert. They're familiar with those characters and the whole Sesame Street world. I familiarized them with it so in the future, when it comes time for them to show it to their kids, they can pass the show onto them.

Captain Bruce Davis Jr.

*I think we hit it off right at the very, very top in terms of our
sensibilities. I think we both recognized in each other good
Midwesterners with the sensibility of Midwest. We were a couple
of kids from farms—Loretta from Paw Paw and me from Grand
Ridge, Illinois. I grew up on a real farm and so did she. I think
there was kind of an immediate bond and link because we were
not coming from the Yale or Harvard with an East Coast
mentality. The people we dealt with in the beginning were some
pretty incredible folks—really major ivy leaguers, like Jon Stone
from Yale and Jerry Lesser from Harvard. Not that we felt
intimidated, but I think we just realized that we were coming from
a different place. I think we had a very same vibe going on in the*

very beginning. It was just a playful, wonderful kind of experiment and none of us knew where it was going to go. It was kind of giddy and kind of thrilling at the same time.

In the very early days of the show I went on tour with Loretta and it was a terrific. I had never done that kind of a tour before. I had toured in Japan and other places, but this was a little different kind of thing. A couple of things stand out from that tour—we went to all the major U.S. cities. One of them was a big concert in a park in Los Angeles. On that tour was Matt Robinson, Loretta, myself, and Big Bird doubling as Oscar of course. That was kind of thrilling because it was the first time I think we had gone out as a small cast, just the four of us, and we saw firsthand how people connected to the show. The tour was a wonderful experience and a highlight of our first and second years on the show. I had an incredible time. Those two years were very special.

After that Loretta and I toured together. That was extraordinary. We toured from Hawaii all the way across this country. I think it must have lasted over a month.

When I think of why we have had the longevity we have had on the show, my head goes in a couple of ways. You don't want to come off as an ego trip saying, because I'm better than anybody else that's been out there doing this. I think there are a lot of factors to it. First of all, I always credit the two years worth of research they did on the show. Sesame Street is the most highly researched television show in history. So much research went into it before our five pilot shows were made. After that only three out of the four of us survived and the original Gordon didn't make it to the pilot episode everyone saw on television.

That's when Matt came in of course. I attribute some of our longevity to that. I also attribute it to the gang of four or five Sesame Street architects, including Jon Stone who was just super bright. He could anything from direct, write, produce—you name it, he could do it. Then there was Dave Connell who came from the Captain Kangaroo Show and was equally as talented as Jon Stone. They had all of the essential skills that were needed to put together a successful show. They were all very intelligent and, put together with the creativity of Jim Henson, they were unstoppable.

That all set the foundation as to why we are still on after forty-five years. The fact that we had the opportunity to audition, and that we passed the audition, and that we got on the show is amazing. God only knows what brought all that together. During the first year of the show, right before the first season started, I came home and I found out that I had been invited to be part of the cast. I wondered who I was supposed to be on this show because up until that time I always thought that people doing anything but concerts were actors.

I had done a minimal amount of acting prior to **Sesame Street.** *I had done some occasional things, some off Broadway, maybe, six or seven summer stocky types of shows. And there was a minimal amount of acting there. I had fortunately gone to HB Studios after I finished my Japan tours because I didn't know what I was going to be doing after that and I thought I'd better have a little training. I asked the producers, who am I supposed to be? They kept avoiding the answer. I was the music teacher and Loretta was Gordon's wife and eventually a nurse. I never really had an identity.*

Susan and Gordon had 1-2-3 Sesame Street, their apartment. Mr. Hooper had his store. I had a 4x8 sheet of plywood—that I had to be hoisted up to—that looked out over Mr. Hooper's store. That was my apartment. I had a door, but I didn't really have an apartment, that was just my pretend apartment. I never got a straight answer as to who I was supposed to be portraying in this show. That went through the whole first year. I kind of kept asking the producers. They said, "well, you know, we'll work it out," or "we'll see."

It was into the second year when I said, "you know, I still don't really know who I'm supposed to be." They said, "we really don't want you to be anybody except yourself." I remember saying to my wife, "they're not going to pay me for just going and being myself. That's not what actors get paid for." I think Loretta and I really did portray these characters by just being ourselves. What they wanted was somebody authentic, that was credible, that could relate to the kids. Loretta was incredible at both singing and acting with the kids. She had a sharp sense of humor. She certainly had a connection to our target audience, which was African American at that point, just by being who she was.

But it came with not having grown up in the East and not having gone to Harvard or Yale or Princeton or something. It came from just having a good Midwestern sensibility. I have always valued that. I think that's why we are both still on the show. On the show, actors have come and gone over the years, quite a number of them actually. They've had people come in an out over the years.

During the 25th season they've practically doubled the cast with some wonderful actors and actresses. However, many of them didn't last.

I was told by somebody that kids can tell when someone is acting or when they are just really speaking honestly and directly to them. I think that Loretta and I both have that kind of down-home sensibility not to come on as professional actors with ten years of Broadway behind us. We just played ourselves and it's worked for a very long time and I'm so grateful for it!

Bob McGrath, Bob on Sesame Street, 1969-Present

Loretta is absolutely one of the most generous, thoughtful, and loving persons that I've ever been associated with.

Working on a show like **Sesame Street** *was such a shock to my system. First of all, the fact that I was actually hired for the job was a major shock. I came from playing all these sometimes not-very-nice characters but, evidently, Jon Stone and Dave Connell saw something in me that they thought I could bring to the role of Gordon. I was thrilled to get the job. Honestly, it was just such a great opportunity. At first, I was really kind of intimidated by having to act with Muppets. I had never even played with dolls before and now here I am talking to and having relationships with these characters on the ends of these puppeteers' arms. It was really very strange, but Loretta and the rest of the cast just really showed me the way.*

In addition to learning to work with the Muppets and the rest of the cast, Loretta and I began to embark on doing personal appearances. This was something that was totally new to me, even more of a departure from anything I'd done before than acting on a T.V. show. I was so incredibly grateful to Loretta for really showing me the ropes and helping me to understand how this really enhanced the mission of **Sesame Street.** *By going out and meeting these families all over the country, we were able to extend the influence of the show. We had so much fun and it was such a* *awakening to me about the impact of* **Sesame Street***. I started to realize that we really were touching the lives of millions and millions of families all over the country and all over the world.*

It was just a labor of love that became such an important part of who I had become by then. After a few years, it was like I had been doing it all my life. Of course, I have Loretta to thank for that because I had no idea that that kind of opportunity was even on the table. To actually use what we were doing to teach children worldwide was a gift that we got from doing **Sesame Street***. It added a whole other dimension to the work, and the fulfillment that we got from the work was amazing. Having that kind of interaction with the audience gave us the opportunity to see how our work on the show touched their lives.*

When I think about the groundbreaking portrayal of Gordon and Susan, I realize that it was part of the original intention of **Sesame Street***. This was almost fifteen years before The* **Cosby Show** *aired. We portrayed a stable, loving African-American couple that were husband and wife, who were both professional people who loved each other, who supported each other, and who were part of this community. This was a rainbow community of people, and Muppets and children. Gordon and Susan were the anchor. We were the married couple. We represented something* *that was so incredibly important and it just felt so natural.*

Loretta and I really were able to convey this in a way that comes from the generosity of spirit that Loretta has. It just permeates everything that she does. It was such an honor, on one hand, but such a pleasure to go to work with her. For me, it's not even like going to work. I'm just going to hang out with our friends. Nothing compares to the love in the sense of family that exists with those who work on the show. When visitors come to our set, they feel it. Frist of all, they come in tears because they grew up watching, and they can't believe that they're actually in the neighborhood where they grew up. They start crying. There's nothing else like it. There's nothing like what "Sesame Street" is and what it represents.

Roscoe Orman, Gordon on Sesame Street, 1974-Present

Growing up in the early 80s I spent every day watching Sesame Street. *I could not wait to practice counting with Count von Count, seeing what Cookie Monster would try to eat, watching Big Bird's adventures and seeing all of the different color monsters and animals flash before my eyes on my rabbit antenna television set. I vividly remember how seamlessly the human characters interacted with the puppets and the many lessons I learned about colors, shapes and different cultures from watching Susan, Mr. Hooper, Maria, Gordon and the many other regulars of my childhood. Looking back as a child, I remember singing, "These Are the People in My Neighborhood" at the top of my lungs annoying my parents and my own neighbors. I distinctly remember Susan working as a nurse as well as helping several of the characters on the show by fixing their cars. As a young girl, I was never really the domestic type, and as I grew older* Sesame Street *showed me that it was okay to be a woman and enjoy helping my dad fix his car—just like Susan! When I watch* Sesame Street, *I honestly do not remember focusing on the character or actor's color or race, just the lessons that were taught. The lessons of making friends, treating others the way that you want to be treated and showing respect was something that traveled across races and cultures. It was important and meaningful to everyone no matter your economic status, your religious background or your race. I remember friends that I*

could count on every day to teach me something new and exciting.
Thirty years later as an assistant principal in the same school in
which I grew up, I still value the lessons learned in my Sesame
Street *watching days. Basic and lifelong lessons are still taught*
on the show, and many of the same loving characters are still a
part of this show's longevity. With so many other choices for
children's shows on television and other methods of media, it is a
difficult market to keep a child's attention for long. However,
with the long achieving success of Sesame Street, *parents of my*
generation turn to what they trust and know first. Every student
that walks through the doors of my school has seen and or can
identify with at least one character on Sesame Street. *It is with*
fond and loving memories that I look back on this part of my
childhood and softly hum, "These Are the People in My
Neighborhood" while walking the halls of Tinicum Elementary
School.

Stephanie Farmer, Assistant Principal, Tinicum School,
Pennsylvania

27637388R00128

Made in the USA
Columbia, SC
04 October 2018